AGRICULTURAL EXTENSION IN CHANGING WORLD PERSPECTIVE

Agricultural Extension in Changing World Perspective

Dr. R.K. SAMANTA

UPPAL PUBLISHING HOUSE
NEW DELHI—110002

UPPAL PUBLISHING HOUSE
3, Ansari Road, Daryaganj, New Delhi-110002

First Edition 1991
ISBN 81-85565-00-7

Printed in India

Published by B.S. Uppal, Uppal Publishing House
3, Ansari Road, Daryaganj, New Delhi-110002
Printed at Sainion Printary, Delhi - 11 00 32.

Dedicated to

Several Hundred Thousands Agricultural Extension Personnel Throughout the World

Foreword

In the post—Second World War II, when production of adequate quantities of food, fibre and other essential agricultural commodities assumed paramount importance in the developing countries of the world including India, agricultural extension gradually became an important factor in the production system. With gradual development of extension organisation and acceptance of extension methodology, there has been a substantial achievement in agricultural production of the country as a whole, but after four decades of organised extension work, in this country, as well as in others we are now faced with some questions challenging the effectiveness and of the approaches made so far. The present situation has been created due to concentration on resource based farmers on irrigated tracts with capital intensive technological options for a few crops. This approach has led to social inequality by creating pockets of prosperity covering hardly thirty percent of the area, while seventy percent constituting primarily marginal and small farmers has to operate under constraints of extremely limited capital resource base, traditional modes of operation, low productivity of the land and abundance of family labour. Life of millions of small and marginal farmers is neither satisfying nor decent. Besides serious doubt has been raised whether results achieved through such capital intensive technology based crop as centred extension approach can be sustained in future. Hence for sustainable agricultural production, agricultural extension is required to reorient its concept and change its approach. Besides sustainability and increase in productivity it is necessary to bring about equality to reduce regional or group imbalances.

To achieve this objective, emphasis has to be given on generation of appropriate technology through participatory research. The aim is to develop a basket of choices available to the complex, diverse and risk prone agriculture in the developing countries of the world. Extension can contribute considerably in this respect by helping the scientists to develop knowledge of the resource poor farmers and their indigenous technical know-how and by analysis of agro-ecosystem—technology interdependence.

Demands put on agricultural extension in the immediate future needs increase in the effeciency of extension functionaries. In this context training plays a vital role. Besides the lacunae that are existent, need to be removed namely lack of linking up of training to varied resource situation of the farmers, lack of insight into social and economic aspects of farming systems, lack of relevancy to the job entrusted and training basically crop oriented rather than farming system oriented.

The situation also needs increasing receptivity of client groups. Any extension effort directed towards development operates through two mutually dependent and interacting mechanism namely the delivery and receiving/utilizing mechanisms. For resource poor villagers along with delivery mechanism equally important are also receiving/utilizing mechanisms, as they constitute client group. It has been felt that in such cases group approach or small group structure is needed for giving the poorer sector a group personality, initiative and bargaining power, as the priorities of the disadvantaged small people differ from the community as a whole.

Dr. R.K. Samanta has been engaged in researches on extension approach and methodology for nearly two decades. In this volume, he has made a sincere attempt to discuss the present day problems of extension and possible methods to make extension strategy more purposive and pervading to bring about development with sustainability and equality. In the present book, due care has been taken of the different facets of the task that lie ahead in view of the situation and problems narrated above.

In U.S.A. evaluation of extension strategy is made every 10 years and plans for future years are made accordingly. In India, no such rigid system is followed, though changes has been made periodically to meet the demands of changing circumstances. In this present book, the author has reviewed the situations existent in developing countries including India and has made constructive suggestions to remedy the defects and present an alternative system for the future.

For this purpose, the book has been suitably divided into six chapters which have dealt the entire gammut of extension strategy for the future. Dr. Samanta has aptly discussed the current agricultural scenario in India from extension view point and has put forward agricultural extension for 21st century. From his experience in extension work, Dr. Samanta has been able to present a clear and composite picture of agricultural extension in present day and the needs for the future.

For a better world which will aim in removing economic disparity between different levels and reducing the poverty in the rural sector, agricultural production system has to be reoriented and augmented which will also require reorientation of agricultural extension in function and structure.

The present volume has dealt these aspects in and effecient manner, and will provide for thoughts and suggestions for planning and executive agencies. It is hoped that this volume will serve the purpose for which it is intended.

Calcutta,
3rd October, 1990.

S.B. Chattopadhyay
Ex-Vice Chancellor
Bidhan Chandra Krishi
Viswavidyalaya,
West Bengal

Preface

Many problems that confront humankind today—war, poverty, hunger, pollution, race relations—are so inter-related that it is difficult to single out one as being more important than others. Some people, however, think that hunger is the greatest of all problems.

Hunger, certainly ranks as one of the oldest human problems. To remove the poverty and reduce the hunger through out the world, enough substantive measures have been taken over the years particularly since middle of this century. Definitely, the agricultural productivity has been tremendously increased over the last four decades or so. But one thing is to be believed today that : 'the world has a problem of hunger but not problem of food'. Infact, many countries show that increasing food does not mean decreasing hunger. Therefore, the crux of the problem is shortage of available income and purchasing power by millions of people, through out the world, who suffer in not getting enough food for their survival.

Now, with the changing agricultural scenario and perspectives in the world the time is ripe for making the need based appropriate extension strategy by which information on food production technology may be transmitted to all the potential users who can adopt those and produce food for their consumption and make available for others. Also income generation and other development programmes are required to be launched simultaneously so that almost all the people of the Third World are able to purchase to meet their basic needs.

The present volume is a sincere attempt by the author to deal with the aforesaid problems to make effective agricultural extension strategy for agricultural development. The volume is divided into six chapters namely :

I. Agricultural Knowledge Transfer—Key for Agricultural Development ;

II. Agricultural Extension in Changing World Perspective ;

III. Agricultural Development Strategy Vis-A-Vis Agricultural Extension Programmes for the Future;

IV. Community Development Strategy and Sociological Perspective of Agricultural and Rural Development;

V. Role of of Extension and Training for Agricultural and Rural Development; and

VI. Agricultural Extension Challenges in India-What can be done ? with detailed expositions on the subjects.

The volume is expected to be of much help to Teachers, Students, Researchers, Development Planners and Administrators, Agricultural Extension and Communication Personnel concerned to agricultural and rural development of the developed and developing countries.

The author would like to express his sincere gratitude to Dr. S.B. Chattopadhyay, a noted agricultural scientist, development administrator and Ex-Vice Chancellor of B.C. Agricultural University, West Bengal, India, who has kindly contributed a "Foreword" to this volume.

A Sincere expression of gratitude goes to Dr. K.V. Raman, Director and Dr. Jagdesh C. Kalla, Jt. Director of National Academy of Agricultural Research Management for their invaluable encouragement in writing this book.

The author is also thankful to M/s Uppal Publishing House for publication of this book in a shortest possible time and Ms. Mita and Mr. Kumar for neatly typing the manuscript of this book.

The author assumes responsiblity for the errors and incorectness of any statement included in this volume. Suggestions for improvement in future editions of this book are most welcome.

Hyderabad, (*India*) R.K. SAMANTA

Introduction

Agricultural extension is a part of the technology transfer system which is primarily concerned whith transmitting information and knowledge of important agricultural technology from research to farmer. As with research, extension requires adequate human and financial resources with the technical and management skills and knowledge associated with new technology to be disseminated to farmers. There is a myth that good technology will spread by references among farmers by word of mouth. There is no doubt that farmer to farmer diffusion is important but extension organisation is essential to accelerate this process and to make sure that an appropriate and valid technology is being disseminated.

Access to agricultural technology presumes that the national agricultural research sub-system has developed and adapted an appropriate technology for farmer use. Weak linkages between research and extension is recognised as probably the most serious institutional problem that constrains the flow of technology to farmers in many countries. The causes of the problem are multifacet, and include such factors as seaprate institutional housing, separate budgets, work plans and attitudinal problems, caused by social, cultural, economic and educational gaps between research and extension personnel. There should be continuous and regular interaction between research and extension personnel including visits to research stations by extensionists, joint on-farm trials, demonstrations and field days, training and workshops given by researcher or research scientists for field extension workers and joint meetings to finalise recommendations, discuss problems and plan joint activities for next agricultural operation.

Since, extension is an educational system, the knowledge and skill level of its professional personnel is of prime importance. The success or failure depends largely on having adequate number and mix of competent extension personnel. Thus, the level of education, training and experience of extension administrators/supervisors, subject matter specialists and field extension staff all are important in assessing the adequacy of extension's human resources.

Good personnel management is also essential because the field staff is widely dispersed, its task is educational, and personal initiative, especially on the part of the frontline personnel, is required for programme success. Many extension programmes in developing countries have administrative policies and procedures which have negative impact on employee morale and thereby limit an extension system performance.

Further, the amount of time extension workers spend on educational and related technology transfer activities in contrast to non-extension duties is an important factor in assessing extension performance. In nearly all developing nations, extension field agents are responsible for a range of non-educational duties imposed by the Government such as Government regulatory work, census, compilation and implementation of credit programmes. These things definitely hamper the agricultural development activities to be performed by the extension agents.

The outputs of extension are the messages disseminated to the farm population. Since messages themselves, can not be measured, attention is shifted to the number and type of extension activities completed in the three general categories of individual, group and mass media methods, which can be used in various combinations tailored to the needs and resources of a country. A number of measures are used to evaluate the dissemination strategy and output of an extension system. These measures examine extension activities occuring at the individual, group and mass media level as well as the capacity of extension to produce its own teaching materials, farmer handouts and materials for electronic media. The ability of the clientele to utilise specific dissemination techniques is also examined.

Keeping all these in mind the author has attempted in a modest way in this volume to present a composite picture of Agricultural Extension needs to meet the agricultural development challenges in coming decades highlighting various facets of agricultural extension with its indepth analyses in six chapters.

The First chapter of the book has emphasised the need of knowledge information and technology interface for sustainable development in agriculture with the support of research-extension linkage. The second chapter has highlighted the need of special agricultural extension programme and strategy to cope up with the changing world agricultural scenario. It has also stressed the needs of communication support and effecient methods and/or models for effective agricultural extension programmes. Chapters three and four have dealt with agricultural and community development strategies focussing indigenous knowledge use and participatory communication for agricultural development actions; and sociological perspective of technology generation in agriculture for rural development respectively. Chapter five has outlined the roles of agricultural and rural development objectives with effective organisational support and possible solutions to its constraints. The sixth and last chapter specifically has dealt with the problems of Indian agricultural extension, raising several research, extension, policy, organisational and management issuse to meet the future challenges.

It is expected that this volume will meet the varying needs of different clientele—agricultural students, teachers and researchers; agricultural extension workers and farmers; policy makers and development administrators; and also will help promote the cause of agriculture and rural development in the world.

R.K. SAMANTA

Contents

ONE

Agricultural Knowledge Transfer : Key for Agricultural Development

Many psychologists and social scientists believe that knowledge brings desirable changes in human behaviour. That behavioural change may be in people's attitude, belief, skill, understanding and perception. But knowledge is the main theme for any type of change to be brought about in individuals' mind. For the farmers, the agricultural knowledge which is influenced by so many factors is important for his understanding and behaviour in decision making in his farming practices. This Chapter, therefore, tries to highlight the different aspects and peripheral areas concerning agricultural knowledge system which in turn helps and influences agricultural decision making by the farmers in micro level and agricultural development in macro level by national planners and development agencies and/or Government.

Further, knowledge generation, transformation, accumulation and utilisation have been the mechanism for human survival. The predominance and control eversince "the purely biological" phase of evolutian had reached its upper limit and natural selection was no longer capable of any advancement." The new method of evolutionary transformation which became available was the transfer and transformation of "tradition" (Huxley, 1957).

Given the fundamental role of knowledge in human survival, it is surprising that the study of knowledge and its utilization has taken such a long time to emerge as a research focus. Suffice it to say that diffusion (e.g. Rogers, 1962, 1971, 1983), utilisation (e.g. Havlock, 1969; Beal *et al.* 1986) and other knowledge processes are now receiving increasing attention. The emergence of new media and information technology have also greatly stimulated the interest. The study of agriculture plays an important role because it provides a dramatic case of knowledge processes in action (Lionberger, 1986).

Keeping all these in view this Chapter has been designed to discuss in details about "Agricultural Knowledge Transfer—Key for Agricultural Development" with five specific dimensions namely :

1. Knowledge, Information and Technology Interface.
2. Technology-Backed Development.
3. Sustainable Development in Agriculture.
4. Research-Extension Linkage for Knowledge Transfer in Enhancing Agricultural Productivity; and
5. Factors Influencing Research and Extension Linkages : Indian Experience.

1. Knowledge Information and Technology Interface

Knowledge is seen as a property of the mind. Knowledge processes (memory storage, transformation, etc.) are intra-personal. Knowledge as such can not be transmitted to others. It can not be seen, heard, smelled or touched, unless transformation are encoded into something else. Knowledge has atleast the instrumental function of providing a "cognetic map" which ensures "correspondence between what the world is perceived to be, and what it terms out to be, when one acts within it to experience some intended consequences (Cantril, 1965). This admittedly limited view fits well with the emphasis on control of the environment.

Information has been designed as a "difference in matter-energy which effects on certainty in a situation where choices exist among a set of alternatives" (Rogers and Kincaid, 1981). Information, is, therefore, a relative concept, depending upon the uncertainty perceived by its receiver. Data are stimuli to the sensory organs. Information is pattern imposed on data which effects the interpretation of those data. Information can be transmitted by imposing such pattern. That is, knowledge can be encoded into information and vice-versa. Purposefully, encoding of information is a risk business because one never knows what will be informative to the intended receiver.

This view of difference between knowledge and information fits the theory of the communication process, meanings are in people. They can be encoded into messages by the sources, and must again be decoded by a receiver to have meaning (Berlo, 1960).

Further, in this regard, technology has interesting connotation and meaning. Technology "is a design for instrumental action that reduces uncertainty in cause-effected relationships involved in achieving a desired out come" (Rogers, 1983). It effects the transmission of inputs and outputs (Fresco, 1986). It is the total of hardware and software for controlling environment for human purposes. The software consists of methods, information, and skills related to the use of a technology. The hardware (tools, equipment, genetic material, etc.) incorporates the technology in a physical object. Technology development can be based upon advancement of science and hence, on application of research findings. However, this is by no means the only method. Technology is continuously developed as a local process of farmers in kitchen, in factories and so on by farmers, extension workers, house wives, labourers and so on.

Since technology serves a human purpose, science cannot lead to technology development in the absence of a human purpose. Hence, technology development takes place along the science-practice continuum. This is the fundamental purpose of any Agricultural Knowledge Information System (AKIS).

Now question comes how this AKIS can be linked or incorporated in other social systems which are the influencing factors for development of knowledge in individuals' mind or in a social system. Following analysis may be viewed as answers to these questions.

In modern society, many sectors exist beside agriculture, in which, the timely delivery of an appropriate knowledge and technology is of crucial importance for survival, be it through innovation, development, maintenance, prevention, adoption, reinforcement, or sustenance. Large multi-national companies and other private and public sectors come in mind first in this regard. They try to set ahead of the competiton by vigorous support of R & D and 'technology transfer' within the company. Usually, they have elaborate institutional structures for supporting product development in special laboratories and by associated companies. They invest heavily in "knowledge system management" to ensure proper functioning of the knowledge information system which supports innovation.

In this connection, Elliott (1987) has proposed a model of the agricultural technology management system (ATMS) which takes the above factors and their influence on the Agricultural Knowledge Information System into account. In his model, he refers the technology sector, what we have called Agricultural Knowledge Information System. The techhology sector contains the 'technology utilising system', the technology generating system, and the technology transfer system. Roling (1989) has replaced Elliott's 'technology sector' with Agricultural Knowledge Information System (Fig.1).

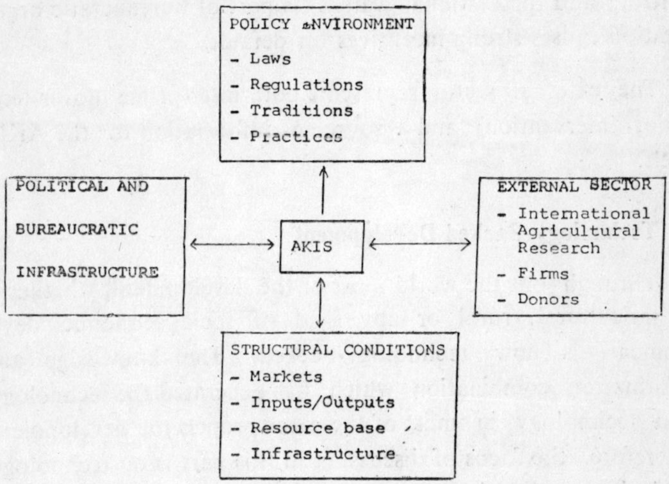

Fig. 1. The Agricultural Technology Management System

Elliott (1987) says, the policy environment plays a crucial role. In some models of AKIS policy is therefore, considered one of the components of the system itself. In his paper, Elliott (1987) treated policy as a prime mover outside the AKIS. Together with two prime movers inside, management and user control policy is considered as a dynamic which can overcome the default incentives which move the AKIS away from synergy, responsiveness, flexibility, relevance and other desired states (Sims and Leonard, 1988).

Likewise, structural conditions play an important role. Thus, variability in the production environment and heterogenity of farmers has tremendous implications for the design and management of the AKIS and its consequences. The assemble of the development mix by farmers requires that technology development and information transfer be coordinated with other elements of the mix, such as seed and input distribution, infrastructure and others.

The political and bureaucratic infrastructure forms a crucial aspect of the AKIS's environment. Often the very fact that the AKIS with its inherent need for farmer orientation, user control, and professional values is part of bureaucratic organization causes strong incentives for default.

The external sector represents both inter-prime mover (e.g. donor intervention) and a source of information for the AKIS itself.

2. Technology-Backed Development

Through out the world most of the development, whether it is agricultural, rural or any kind of social/economic development, is now technology-backed. The knowledge and information combination which has generated the technology, that technology in most of the cases propels the development. Therefore, the focus of discussion in this part is on technology-backed agricultural development.

Another aspect of technology-backed development is the direct linkage between scientists (the technology developers) and farmers (the technology users). Effective research and development by and with resource poor farmers require understanding and interactions of many types and at many stages. This includes social relationships, exchange of ideas and information, linkage between people and institutional dimensions. The interactions—between researchers and farmers, between extension workers and farmers, between women and men and between outside science and technology and local capacities must be considered for technology development and its dissemination to the users of technology.

The importance of the farmer-scientist link for development of technology has been widely accepted through out the world today. It not only enhances the compatibility and viability of technology developed by the researchers but also increased the rate of adoption by technology users. It also improves the relationship between the two for effective R & D programmes to benefit the rural people. Farmer groups and workshops are one useful way to help elicit farmers' ideas to improve communication and to foster local initiatives. The farmer-scientist link can be a good means of overcoming the barriers between them and some times extensionists.

Agricultural development requires a "mix" of conditions (Haverkort & Roling, 1984). Although the precise nature of the mix depends on the context, it usually indicates a good infrastructure, access to credit, water, land, markets, relevant technology and rewarding prices (Mosher, 1966). As agriculture develops, the mix of requirements is increasingly satisfied. In other words, an unsotisfactory mix no longer impades innovation. The greater the control, which farmers have over their environment, the more important knowledge and technology become as the major determinants of development (Jiggins, 1988). And as a result, technology-propelled or technology-backed development takes off. It is no doubt a specific diffusion mechanism.

Technology-backed development implies that one must set ahead of the game if one is to set in business. This holds for individual farmers, regions and nations. A country which allows its agricultural industry to fall behind must count on relatively cheap imports squeezing out local farming or it must rise protective barriers. A country which wants to export agricultural products must keep its competitvie edge.

Another benefit of technology-backed development, is that the promotion of agricultural technology utilization requires relatively little attention. In agriculture, a relatively high effort can lead to rapid difiusion process, especially because of the prices feedback loop which gives the diffusion process a satisfactory character. As a result, one finds farmers at the forefront so given for the new ideas that they exert strong pressure on the AKIS for new ideas.

3. Sustainable Development in Agriculture

Agricultural development is no longer a means to end hunger and scarcity. What it does in a context of glut is to reallocate resources and essentially access to scarce markets to areas and people who can produce more efficiently. Agricultural development, in the absence of countervailing measures, has high costs in terms of the numbers of people whose livelihoods are effected. Usually, these costs are externalised.

We live in a world in which everyday brings new science that our environment is deteriorating around us. Evidence that this downward trend has been brought to halt or even reversed is scarce. Some major threats are salination, erosion, resistance of pests and diseases to control measures, soil exhaustion deforestation and desertification, surface and ground water pollution, poisioning and flooding, etc.

Man's dramatically increased capacity to exert an influence on the environment "has created a new need. The need for something which neither pure science—aimed at increasing our understanding of the natural world—nor technology, aimed at controlling it. We now need to understand what we are doing to the world and how our actions in one or effect other, apparently quite remote areas." (Clarke, 1985).

Professionals, therefore, in agricultural development, are greatly realising that modern agricultural science and technology have a certain bias which cause a different impact on development in different regions and areas. Due to the growth of the population the low price for agricultural produce, structural changes, nomadic and sedementary agriculture as well as apparent short term success of introduction of modern technologies and its appeal to study the more professional systems no longer seem to satisfy the needs of the people.

And it is evident today that agricultural systems are rapidly changing in the search to marry a dwindling (per capita) and deteriorating resource base, higher output requirements and decreasing agricultural prices. Development of a more sustainable agriculture has become a high priority for many Governments in the world today.

Sustainable development can only take place through an integrated approach as starting point. Therefore, an understanding of the present framing and land use system and its development over time is necessary. This has to be combined with the limitations and possibilities of the natural eco-system as well as with a study of the agricultural knowledge and experience of the farming population. The understanding of the present situation should contain assessments of the potentials for agricultural development, available physical, biological and human resources. It should also take into account the political, social, cultural and economic context of the agricultural system, such as the different roles of men and women, available technologies, extension structure and production costs and benefits.

The present situation can be supplemented with the principles of ecological agriculture and findings of modern agricultural science and research as illustrated below (Fig. 2).

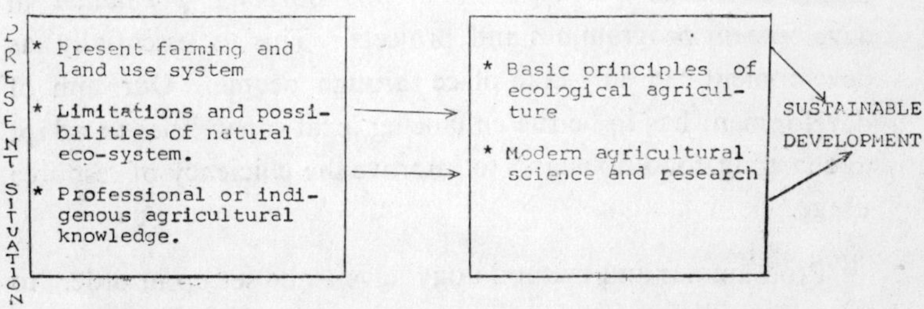

Fig. 2 : Sustainable Development in Agriculture

However, as a farming system, ecological agriculture is based in the continuous balancing between production demands and respect for the eco-system. Primary aim is the realisation of high and lasting soil fertility as a basis of sustainable production and development. Ecological agriculture is site-oriented and puts on farm researches to its full use, thereby, creating a minimal tendency of external inputs. In its approach, ecological agriculture is clearly distinct from conventional and traditional agriculture.

Conventional agriculture is essentially market oriented and mainly aims at a maximum financial returns. In this intensive use is made of external inputs such a chemical fertilizers, biosides, high yielding varieties and mechanisation. Whereas, *traditional* agriculture is subsistence oriented in its pure form as practiced before being externally influenced, it uses low level of locally available inputs and is characterised by its stability and high sustainability.

In this regard, the most common agricultural system found now-a-days in developing countrise can be classified as a mixture of conventional and traditional agriculture. In some cases, more towards the traditional side, in other cases having many characteristics of conventional agriculture. But, a blend of the both possibly will produce better result.

An important condition for sustainable agricultural development is the *participation of the farming population* in development programmes and projects. This is essentially as development can only take place through people. Our aim of development has to be the enhancing local capabilities to adapt to changing conditions and to improve the efficiency of resource usage.

Programmes and methodology have to be set up in order to stimulate and support farmers to organise themselves and to activate their role in technology development. This emphasized recognition of the importance of indigenous knowledge of the farming population. Beside knowledge of land, soil, water and their inter-relations, this also has to include an information on infrastructure and social, cultural, political and religious aspects. This approach requires a re-orientation of the role of researchers and extension workers. They will have to perform a function that complements farmers' existing knowledge rather than replacing.

Practically, this asks for participatory technology development (Haverkort, *et al*, 1988) in which farmers and research/extension workers cooperate in the efforts to improve technology. This implies an acceptance that farmers can, to a large extent identify and modify their own solutions to their own needs. Therefore, the target population should be involved in a policy formulation and decision making right from the beginning. Government agencies and bureaucratic forces are often reluctant towards participation. The rural population faces socio-cultural restrictions in speaking on equal terms in open meetings with officials and educated development workers. Over coming these problems will take a lot of energy, endurance and creativity. However, it is only by this approach that we can realise our ultimate aim of empowerment of social groups towards access and control the other resources and decision making.

Lastly, considering the above principle in agriculture, it may be said that ecological farming practices for sustainable development are site-specific and can not be simply copied into any environment. However, certain general characteristics will be there. They are :

1. The system is modeled on the natural eco-system of the area and indigenous flora and fauna are used as much as possible.
2. The land-scape is mosaic patterned following the contour lines and soil type patterns. Patches of forest are linked up by windbreaks, thus, framing the land-scape in a network of trees.
3. Nutrients are recycled, within the farming as well as of a landscape level.

4. Pest and disease control is based on prevention through farm design and management.
5. There is a great diversity in plant and animal life. Single elements in the farming systems are linked together through symbiotic interrelations.
6. Planning takes place on a long term basis in order to create production stability. There is a trend towards including more perannuals in the system.

These knowledges are basic keys for ecological agriculture for sustainable development and must be transmitted for wider use with an eye to achieve higher productivity and growth in agriculture.

4. Research-Extension Linkage for Knowledge Transfer in Enhancing Agricultural Productivity

The main objective of both research and extension should be to increase farm productivity and to enhance farm incomes, atleast cost to the farmers. To achieve this objective in ways consistent with nation's productivity the extension system must feed the research workers information about the constraints farmers have experienced in adopting research recommendations, and the research system must have the capacity and readiness to respond with problem specific recommendations. Research should also seek to obtain direct feedback from the field, through field visits undertaken by research scientists, preferably accompanied by extension workers.

Research and extension (R & E) linkages must accommodate the need for seasonal or inter-annual flexibility and adaptation and producer knowledge of local production conditions assumes a higher value. There are two consequences. One is that, given that farmers in high potential areas, who have better control over their production environment, will continue to improve their efficiency, it is not unlikely that they will manage to strive agricultural prices down below the level at which it is feasible for a rainfed producer to use modern inputs find varieties. This implies that maintaining farming in some rain-fed areas would require a technology based on different principles (Hoverkort, 1988).

In many cases, in many countries, the agricultural knowledge information system is administratively divided into a research and extension directorate, department or division. This administrative setup, might or might not, create an adequate infrastructure for effective information exchange. What is important is to distinguish the administrative setup (the formal organisation chart) from the knowledge and information system (Blok & Seegers, (1988).

Usually, the administrative distinction between research and extension leaves an information gap which can not be abridged easily by linkage mechanisms. Their ideologies, self-images and professional ethics are often very different (Bennett, 1988). Extension waits for readymade technologies and recommendation and focused on networking and service, while research emphasise scientific publications, which are half finished products from the point of view of extension. McDermott, (1987) points out that some instructional go-betwcen, a subject matter specialist or technical liaison and support is necessary to abridge the gap. In this middle ground, there is no way to clearly distinguish research and extension.

According to McDermott, (1987), the functions of these go-between are :

1. Maintain liaison with research so as to keep abreast of new technical developments and help translate field problems into researchable questions;
2. To establish linkages with input suppliers to improve the chances that the right inputs will be available; and
3. To provide technical support to field staff and pick up field problems from them.

Important functions of technical liaison are adaptive research, training, developing the reference material and training aids, trouble shooting and responding to extension agents on requests for help.

Again when the results have been tested in the farmers' fields, then, the extension agents must be able to disseminate it to the farmers. This requires a system with agents capable of understanding the research process, knowing the limits to the research and communicating on a professional level with the researchers. Thus, it emphasized that there must be an intimate professional link between extension and research.

Although, there may be a number of variations, it seems there are two basic models for research and extension systems. In the first, research and extension are in the same Institution. In USA, these two functions are found in the Land Grant Universities, where specialists often have both a research and an extension assignment. They may also teach in the faculty of agricultre. The same systems are well practised presently in all the Agricultural Universities of India. Of course, in United States, recently, extension services are fully looked after by Cooperative Extension Services and the county extension agents. This system assumes that the farmers are well educated, have good communication facilities, are relatively few in number, with large holdings and supported by a viable commercial sector that provides them with the inputs and knowledge.

In the second type of model, the research and extension institutions are separate because of the nature of the agricultural sector, the number of people, and the traditions of the country. This separation does not produce result or achieve desired objective and agricultural productivity as a result, suffers. Both the functions should work in unison to achieve and accomplish desired objectives.

When research and extension are separate, it becomes even more important to transform research results into terms that the extension agents can understand. The linkage between them is a two-way communication from the farmers to the extension agents to the researchers, and then from the researchers to the extension agents, to the farmers. Communication among these three different groups require an understanding of the needs and levels of education of all three.

To promote agricultural development, information must reach the farm level in a usable form. Researcherss, traditionally are not the best equipped to transform their results to a form understandable to the farmers. Therefore, a major role of extension agent is to translate this information into culturally usable recommendations, adapted to the farmers, level of understanding and resources.

This widely held opinion that the linkage between research and extension should be improved-starts off on the wrong foot by suggesting that the problem can be solved by creating effective linkage mechanisms between two different departments. The problem really is to develop a set of cogs so that the required shifts between different speeds can be made and the required transformation can take place. Only, then the linkage mechanisms become important.

Here, it may be mentioned that the institutional go-betweens which abridge the gap between 'Research' and 'Extension' do not only ensure downstream flows, but are specially important for the upstream ones.

5. Factors Influencing Research and Extension Linkages : Indian Experience

The examples and analyses cited above thus far show the range of problems that surface within the effective extension systrm in place and that require a strong research-extension linkage, which is now generally acknowledged as crucial to the success of extension for agricultural development. But in actual practice, linkage is not implemented to an extent commensurate with the general agreement about its necessity. There are so many factors that influence this linkage. Unless these factors are analysed, it is not possible to establish firm and enduring interaction. The linkage should not depend on the chance contact, at the personnel level, between the research scientist and the extension worker, currently deployed at a place. Rather linkage should be an integral part of the system. There are some factors, external to the research extension set up, that influence organisational behaviour of these establishments. Necessary attention must be paid to these factors if a proper environment is to be created for the needed organisational changes within research and extension.

India's past agricultaral performance and the factors mainly responsible for it, generally decide the values placed by policy makers and development administrators on the type of research and the kind of extension services desired. If in the past, professional extension did contribute substantially to achieve a break-through in productton, then there is bound to be a strong commitment to the development of professional extension including the necessary changes in the research and extension set up and the establishment of research-extension linkage can be accomplished without much difficulty. Therefore, the first step in establishing strong research extension linkage is to improve overall understanding of the process of agricultural development and of the role of professional agricultural extension in the context of future challenges. It is also equally important to associate the national political system at all levels with extension. The manner and degree of such association will of course, vary among countries.

However, it is worth mentioning that on research side, early successes were largely attributed to superior genetic varieties that emerged from the research stations. The continuing emphasis of research on Plant breeding is therefore, understandable. There is another reason that scientists are more keen on undertaking research on plant breeding than on soils. For example, it is easier to spread a new promising crop variety among farmers than a message about how to treat the land for scientific dryland farming. The latter requires a professional extension system, whereas the former—particularly, when the varieties are responsive to irrigation, as is often the case can reach the farmers, at least the progressive ones. Thus, the important factors external to the research set up, which largely determine the relative priorities accorded by the research establishment to different disciplines, are the contribution of the different disciplines, to the purpose of agriculture. It is quite clear, that an effective, extension system is an essentially pre-condition to the stimulation of research in certain fields.

The extent to which research workers are associated with long term agricultural planning by development planners and administrators is another important factor. It is necessary for the country's long-term priorities and research gaps to be clearly identified and research scientists should be fully involved in this exercise. It is quite necessary for the scientists to be able to perceive clearly the relevance of their research to the country's long-term agricultural development. In the absence of such an association, emphasis will continue to be on the areas that contributed to the best performance of the agricultural sector.

Therefore, it may be stated, that to develop genuinely substansive linkages between agricultural research and extension, there must be increased emphasis on on-farm research, with special attention to feedback from extension staff and farmers. Such feedback is essential to complement more conventional programmes of experimentation in agricultural research stations, which in the past has been confined to individual crops and livestock and have never taken into account all the economic, social and cultural conditions of the people. Without the support and understanding of the people, who do the farming, the recommendations of such programmes can not and will not be applied. And to be more effective this increased emphasis must be accompanied by greater inter-disciplinary cooperation among researchers, farmers and extension staff working in the field.

To achieve the greater success, in research and extension, linkages for enhancing agricultural productivity of agricultural institutions, policies, and procedures must be more responsive to the interests and needs of all farmers, particularly, to the vast majority who are small and marginal farmers, and at the same time they must be responsive to national economic development goals. These two requirements can be mutually supportive.

References

Beal, G.M. and P. Meehan (1986). Communication in Knowledge Production, Dissemination and Utilisation, In Beal et al (1986) Knowledge Generation, Exchange and Utilisation. Boulder : Westview Press.

Bennett, C. (1988). Improving Co-ordination of Extension and Research through the use of interdependency models. Bologna : 7th International Congress of Rural Sociology, Theme Session on Extension.

Berlo, D. (1960). The Process of Communication. New York : Holdt, Rinehart and Winston.

Blok, K. and S. Seegers (1988). The Research-Extension Linkage in the Southern Region of Sri Lanka. An Agricultural Information Systems Perspective. Wageningen : AUW, Unpublished M. Sc. Thesis.

Cantril, H. (1965). The Pattern of Human Concerns, New Brunswick (NJ) : Rutgers Univ. Press.

Clarke, R. (1985). Science and Technology in World Development, Oxford : OUP and UNESCO.

Elliott, H. (1987). Diagnosing Constraints in Agricultural Technology Management Systems. The Hague : ISNAR, paper for international workshop 7-11 September, 1987.

Fresco, L.O.F. (1986). Cassava and Shifting Cultivation, A Systems approach to agricultural technology development. Amsterdam : Royal Tropical Institute.

Havelock, R.G. (1969). Planning for Innvovation through the Dissemination and Utilisation of Knowledge. Ann Arbor : UOFM : CRUSK.

Haverkort, A.W. and N.G. Roling (1984). Six Rural Extension Approaches. Wageningen : IAC, International Seminar on Strategies for Rural Extension.

Haverkort, B. (1988). Agricultural Production Potentials : inherent or the result of investments in technology development ? Accepted for publication by *Agricultural Administration and Extension.*

Haverkort, B. et. al (1988). Strengthening Farmers' Capacity for Technology Development, ILEIA, Oct. 1988, 4(3), p. 3-7, ETC Foundation, Leusden, The Netherlands.

Huxley, J. (1957). Knowledge, Morality and Destiny. New York : Mentor Books.

Jiggins, J. (1988). Conceptual Overview : how poor women earn income in rural subs-Saharan Africa and what prevents them from doing so. Nairobi : Ford Foundation, Women's Programme Forum : 'Expanding Income Earning Opportunities for Women in Poverty: a Cross Regional Dialogue, held at Intercontinental Hotel, May 1—5, 1988.

Lionberger, H.F. (1986). Towards an Idealised Systems Model for Generating and Utilising Information in Modernising Societies. In Beal, G.M. et al, op. cit.

McDermott, J.K. (1987). Making Extension Eeffective : the Role of Extension/Research Linkages. In Rivera, W. and S. Schram (Eds). op cit.

Mosher, A.T. (1966). Getting Agriculture Moving. New York : Agricultural Development Council.

Rogers, E.M. and L.D. Kincaid (1981). Communication Networks. Towards a New Paradigm for Research. New York : The Free Press.

Rogers, E.M. (1962, 1971, 1983). Diffusion of Innovations. New York Free Press.

Roling, N. (1989). The Research/Extension Interface : A knowledge system perspective, Staff Notes, ISNAR, Netherlands.

Sims, H. and D. Leonard (1988). The Political Economy of the Development and Transfer of Agricultural Technologies. The Hague : ISNAR. Theme Paper for the 'Agricultural Research/ Technology Transfer Interface' Research Project.

TWO

Agricultural Extension in Changing World Perspective

Agricultural Extension is the back-bone and foundation of any type of development in agriculture. Unless the knowledge about agricultural innovation, package of practices and its proper utilisation are transmitted or extended to its users, it has no value at all. Therefore, agricultural extension must be a constituent of any kind of development strategy for agricutural and rural development in any country.

One word of caution must be kept in mind when we talk of agricultural extension. Often, people mix the 'agricultural extension education' with 'extension services.' Again, agricultural research and agricultural extension must go hand in hand to know the problems of the users regarding agricultural knowledge utilisation and incorporation of the same in research projects to find out probable and expected solutions to the problems. The linkage between research and extension, therefore, must be studied to a greater extent for transforming agri-agricultural technology to its users with an eye to achieve agricultural development objectives in the chaning world perspective.

Keeping this in focus, the present Chapter is designed to discuss various dimensions of agricultural extension to achieve allround development goals in three broad heads :

1. Agricultural Extension and its varying dimensions;
2. Communication Support for Extension in Agricultural Development; and
3. Extension Methods and Models for Effective Extension Programmes.

1. Agricultural Extension and its Varying Dimensions

A network of extension organisations spread throughout the nook and corner of the country, has been yoked to the services of rural areas for an allround improvement including agriculture. Notwithstanding the fact that the extension missionary has been the common element in different phases of agricultural development since independence, the word 'extension' has been much more maligned, directly or indirectly, by both the informed and uninformed people alike, than, admire for the delicate roles played all through. Everybody used to talk about extension and it seems extension is just a simple concept and any body can perform the job of extension educator or extension agent easily which is not true. Extension education truly is a profession. The concept and the philosophy behind the term, 'extension education' is well established and pronounced. It is the main theme of education which brings desirable and expected changes in human behaviour. Let us discuss now about the 'extension education' at a length.

Extension Education as a Profession

The first and foremost aspect which attracts our attention is to discuss and decide whether or not extension is a profession. The layman's immediate response would be that it is not. A little reflective thought would, however, make us believe that there is definitely something professional about extension education. The entire superstructure of extension education heavily rests on the desirable change in behaviour complex of the people with whom the work is done. This is by no means an easy task. It calls for a herculean effort on the part of the exetnsion personnel to achieve the objective of desirable change in thoughts and actions of the people. Motivation of the tradition-bound farmers, whose experience has stood the test of time through educational process, demands a band of well groomed community extension personnel.

Profession of Extension Education can grow and develop only when there is a strong base of knowledge of extension education. The erroneous concept of extension education is an informal, out of school system of education, is no more valied now. Formal and informal educations are best methods and not the knowledge itself. Extension Education, infact is applid science. Its main base is technology, which is to be introduced in the system through favourable expenses and adoption by the people. This also necessitates a further understanding of the social system in which the technology is to be introduced. Extension education like any other science has three distinct inter-related wings, i.e., teaching, research and extension services. Unfortunately, most of us consider extension services as the complete concept of extension education. But in reality, it is one third of the total science of extension education.

Further, research in extension education is also an important component for development strategy in agriculture and rural development. Research provides materials for continuous growth and development of any profession. The future of extension education as a profession, therefore, would greatly depend on the quality of knowledge, constantly poured into it. It is distressing that so far the need for research in extension education has not been realised by those who are in the helm of affairs of deciding upon the research strategy for agriculture and rural development. If the profession of extension education is to continue its strive towards bringing about desirable change in the life and living of the farming communities in India, without jeopardising the democratic fabric of the society, researches in extension education are a must. The utility of science lies in the service it can render to the society. To serve the people better, effectively and purposefully, people's needs and problems are to be identified first. And then probable solutions can be evolved and provided to them. And this is only possible through meticulous research on the subjects and areas.

Conflict between Extension Education and Extension Services

Establishment of Agricultural Universities in India in early 60s on the pattern of the Land Grand Universities of the USA, has let loose a cut throat competition between the State Departments of Agriculture and the Agricultural Universities. This competition is uniform all over the country, particulary in the field of extension education. Most of the states of India have transferred the teaching and research responsibilities to the Agricultural Universities. But the future of extension education and its position in the decision making of development plan activities and strategies still hang in air in many states, and in national plrnning procedures. The present confusion and impass are more because of the lack of proper understanding of the concept of extension education than anything else.

In developing countries like India, which is beset with that every chronic paucity of resources, the supply of services and inputs has been tagged on to the extension organizations. A more cogent view, however, would reveal the inadequacy of mixing of the elements of "education" and "supply" in extension organisations. Somehow, it has not been possible to insulate one from the other and more often they seem to be inseparably dovetailed. In advanced countries, however, supply of services and inputs is mostly in the hands of the private institutions and the extension agents are confined to the education knowledge input only. As things stand, it would be impossible to do away with this symbiotic relationship between extension education and extension services for many years to come in India. Nontheless attempts have to be made to avoid dilution of educational input of extension education.

Agricultural Univerities in India are based on the philosophy of integration between teaching, research and extension. Extension, here, stands for extension education and not for supply of services and inputs. Though supply of services and inputs and a host of other regulatory functions would continue to be the main focus of attention of the Department of Agriculture of the State Governments, the educational aspect of extenston education should vest with the Agricultural Universities.

Extension Personnel and Organisational Support for Extension

Agricultural extension has historically been perceived as a function of low status performed by poorly qualified and poorly equipped persons who deal with poor and frequently illiterate farmers in remote rural areas. This perception has been supported by facts : low salaries, unclear job description, poor supervision of performance and poor quality of work by extension personnel.

This situation and working climate of the extension personnel can never be congenial for them to contribute more efficiently in the development process in agriculture. Their role and job description must be well defined and they must be provided with the necessary support and services for their job satisfaction.

Further, regarding the role of extension personnel there is a little misconception found in various countries, particularly, in the third world. This should be clear.

Agricultural communicators define technology transfer as the communication's task of transferring information about new technology from the researcher to the farmer and of transmitting farmers' problems back to the researcher. For agricultural extensionists, although a two-way communciation is essential, technology transfer also involves helping clients learn how to use new technology to achieve their goals. In short, an agricultural communicator would emphasize educating clients to use technology effectively. Agricultural communicators tend to rely more on mass communications, while agricultural extensionists tend to work more with individuals and groups. Agricutural communication makes intensive use of capital while agricultural extension uses more skilled manpower.

The mix of communication and extension needed in a country depends on the nature of the technology being extended, on the farmers, level of technological sophistication, and on the existence of alternative sources of information, including the private sector and farmers' organizations. Agricultural technology can be simple or complex. For example, a new highyielding rice variety can be a simple form of technology if the farmer merely has to substitute one variety for another. Transferring simple technology to farms may be largely a communication task. The farmer does not have to learn new practices or techniques. However, if the farmer needed to learn a new production process, then technology transfer would become a more complex task. A good example would be the discovery of a new rice variety that matures in 90 days instead of 130 days; this would allow the farmer to grow two crops a year instead of one, but to get the second crop the farmer would have to direct seed rather than transplant the first crop. In addition, the farmer might have to change the timing and the rate of fertilizer application for both crops and apply an insecticide on the second crop to control insects. Clearly, transferring more complex forms of technology requires more educational input. In the example of above, there is a need for both communication and extension, particularly extension.

Moreover, the approach to the transfer of any technology varies with the cultural and socio-economic characteristics of the potential clients. For example, farmers in a relatively closed environment tend to rely on more personalised forms of communication, especially with people in whom they have developed confidence. As their environment opens up, their medium of communication becomes less personalised, and they acquire skills to seek and process their own information. Thus, any extension methodology has to recognise the nature of the client's decision-making process and be flexible enough to adjust to changes over time.

Specialised Extension Agency and Technology Transfer

A specialised extension agency has generally been advocated for three reasons :

(1) the staff members would have the opportunity to concentrate on extension, including its communication and education components;

(2) the staff would be relatively homogeneous, which would enable the organization to monitor and evaluate their performance more effectively; and

(3) there would be a high probability that once resources are allocated to extension, they would be used for that purpose.

There are three disadvantages to setting up a specialized extension agency, particularly in those developing countries in which institutions are very weak. First, a specialized agency would require the parallel development of the agencies to perform other technology transfer functions. Secondly it would create a need for coordination among agencies, responsible for technology transfer, on the one hand, and between these agencies and policy makers and planners, on the other. Thirdly, it would increase the competition for scarce manpower resources and funds when resources are insufficient to meet the existing needs of all categories.

An agency made responsible for extension, input supply, and services, has major advantages under special conditions. For example, if an area or a category of farmers needs special development assistance, some or all of the technology transfer activities can be combined in one organization and the size of the staff can be tailored to meet the exact nature of the functions to be performed. The disadvantage of this approach lies in the risk that the relatively less demanding but more visible functions (such as the supply of inputs and services) will distract the attention of the management and the staff from the equally important function of extension, where and when it is required.

The selection of a form of organisation for supporting the technology transfer functions in general, and extension in particular, has to start with a clear definition of the objective and the means available to achieve it. This may be sound obvious, but it was a missing element in all the systems reviewed so far. The objective needs to be specified in relation to time. Thus, a short-term objective (for example, the transfer of a defined technological prectice) should be clear not only the substance, but also how it relates to a longer-term objective (institution building). The two are not mutually exclusive, but they may require different policy decisions and strategies. Of the means available for seeking these objectives, a distinction should be made between desire to make the best possible use of inadequate resources to perform a function and the building of capability to achieve perfection in the performance of that same function in the future. Again, the two alternatives are not mutually exclusive. The first may precede, and even lead into the second.

2. Communication Support for Extension in Agricuttural Development

Information is the basis for decision making, as well as of all aspects connected with the management of agricultural research planning, organising, staffing, motivating and controlling. This vertical set up in the research planning and development information has also to flow from the laboratory to the field, consumers of the results of research, the extension services and through them ultimately to the farmers. Thd public in general should also be able to know what is going on in the crucial field, so vitally important to them in meeting the country's needs. The progress and development and the role research is playing in a twin-achievement have to be clearly brought home to them if they have to fully involved in participating actively in national programmes and efforts.

A rational approach to research planning requires that the planners at the Central, regional and State levels be well informed of national and state requirements, based on what has already gone on, what results have been achieved, and whether the new sites have to be set. Planning at any level needs a systematic collection of information and related reseach both within and outside the research organization, within and outside the country. Science and Technology are truly international and no research scientist can limit his knowledge of research activities to only a limited part of the globe. Thus, research information has to be multi-directional in its flow, and communication, thus becomes a crucial part in the management and utilisation of agricultural research for ultimate development of agriculture.

Extension Information and Scientist as a Communicator

During the last 35 to 40 years, the Scientists in India have been increasingly playing another important role, that of a communicator. Findings in the laboratory and in the experiment fields will not fulfil their objectives unless they reach the consumer of research results. There was a time when the Scientist's function ended when he wrote up the findings of a research project and had it published in scientific journal. But the present day field based and problem oriented research gave him necessarily the functioning of translating the results of consumption by extension specialists and farmers. The extension specialists need all assistance once again in formulating his recommendations and advice to the farmer and there in the Scientist has this additional and important role to perform. The agricultnral scientist who hither really participated in a dialogue with the farmers has now established himself as a reliable communicator and has developed over the last few years a high sense of reliabiliy among his target audiences. Therefore, the scientists must perform the job not only of a researcher but also as an extension communictor to transfer his research findings to its ultimate users.

Further, extension services have also their own organizations concerning the dissemination of information to the frontline communicators. A very thin line divides research information from extension information and the difference is directly in the technique adopted in the presentation of the information to the extension workers and the farmers. This has also given rise to an excellent feedback, enabling the Scientist to bring back to the laboratory problems arising out of his dialogue with farmers and take up research which has immediacy and importance as against the leisurely pace with which research on fundamental aspects of agriculture used to be conducted earlier.

Communication Education and Research Support for Communication

The present pattern of personnel of non-scientific training to handle technical information is beset with danger in transmitting distortions in the communication of information. There is an urgent need to lay emphasis in the communication education and training to the people those who are engaged as extension agents or linkers between research results and the ultimate users of the agricultural technology/information. To this end, it is necessary to provide pre-service, in-service and, professional training in all communication media, Ultimately this country needs to develop a first class frontline agricultural communicators who can takeover the good positions in the communication line at various states and levels. The research support for communication also comes in the picture in overall dimension of communication education to the extension personnel.

This, therefore, is the highlight of the multi-directional and multi-dimensional communciation requirement of the country vis-a-vis agricultural research, starting with feeding of information at the highest levels of administration and planning down to the level of consumers of the end product of research. And awareness regarding communication at all levels of development projects has now come to all countries, what is known as 'development support communication.' What we need today is a 'research support commounication' system.

For this, the importance of communication for fruitful and speedy research has to be fully appreciated, and communication has to be accepted as an essential and in built component of any research project and as a part of the total investment on the project earmarked for communication efforts. Communication efforts, themselves have to be spelt out at each stage of development and implementation of the project, so that the audiences at various levels are identified and a communication programme suitable for each audience will be planned, prepared and implemented.

Lastly, it may be said that organisations for communication to farmers, agri-businesses, research workers and extension agents etc., have been created, equipments provided, persons put in positions and the progress is scientifically known. But till todate, desired results have not been achieved or objectives are not fulfilled. And therefore, there are enormous qualitatives as well as quantitative inadequacies which need to be made good and effective. Unless and until, communication is effective, no amount of technology, training and the persons can bring desirable change in the farmers' behaviour and agricultural development process can not reach its expected heights.

Potential of Communication for Development

One might envisage a system of development support communication in all development fields, catering for the real information needs of the people and of Governments, fostering a genuine two way flow of information. It would definitely be a keystone in a democratic communication system, in which ordinary people would have much greater access to and opportunity to participate in communications: in which individuals and groups enjoyed 'a right to communicate, a right to be informed and a right to inform.' On a more modest level there is enough experience to form with properly and genuinely conceived development support communication can reduce the costs and speed up the pace of planned and beneficial change, helping to boost production in farms/workshops, to improve levels of education, health and nutrition, to stimulate community development and self-help and to contribute to the universally accepted values of equality and participation in development. This contribution, as well as, being recognised in theory should be more fully exploited in practice. It should not be, as it so often is a missing link in the development process. Therefore, development strategy and agricultural production problem must make use of communication input to achieve its desired objectives and goals. To make this understanding more clear following description may be useful.

Most of the old and existing ideas about communication have been derived from what might broadly be described as a Western cultural framework. There is a new awareness of the need among the people in the world for a wider input from different philosophical, sociological, cultural, political and ethical backgrounds to form the basis for a more comprehensive understanding. In the past century there has been a steady rise in world educational and literacy standards. And also there has been a remarkable improvement in people's ability to handle and use equipments/machineries, including the mass media and new communication technologies. As a consequence, more and more people in the world today can read, write and use communication media and can no longer be denied access to and participation in media process for the lack of communication and handling skills. So, by exploiting these resources of the people, the development programme can be designed in such a manner that rural people can be reached effectively and in a less possible time.

Of course, there is an imbalance and disparity in communication resources found in different regions and countries of the world. The disparities between quantitative as well as qualitative communication resources between different parts of the world on the one hand and within the distinct levels of society on the other, is increasingly recognised as a case of concern. Communication policies and planning, therefore, must be formulated in such a manner that it helps redress these imbalances and disparities.

The actual and potential changes in communication may possibly by technology developments necessitates the new statement of communication rights and freedoms. Some communication systems (for example, audio and video taping, copying, radio broad-casting, etc.) have become so cheap and so simple that the rationale for regulating and controling them is no longer relevant. Therefore, the introduction of transister radios and VCRs essentially can be said to be two of the most important developments in mass communication in the post-war world.

Further, the growing sense of trans-nationalisation and cultural synchronisation, perhaps has given the greatest impetus toward a new formulation of communication freedoms and the need for realistic communication policies and planning. This cultural synchronization can take place without perceptible dependent relationship. And this phenomenon has shown trend towards democracy. Though often ignored or only seen at the level of lip service in practice, concepts like freedom, democracy and participation have been spread all over the world. Nevertheless, the communication media are still largely controlled by Governments or powerful private interests. But in the light of the above developments, they are more attuned to and aware of the democratic principles than before.

Modern mass media and alternate networks of folk media or inter-personal communication channels are not mutually exclusive by definition. Contrary to the principles of diffusion theories, they are more effective if appropriately used in an integrated fashion, according to the needs and constraints of local context. The modern mass media having been mechanically transplanted from abroad into the Third World societies, enjoy varying and limited rates of penetration. However, they can be effectively combined providing a functional division of labour is established between them and provided the limits of the mass media are recognised.

Lastly, witnessing and experiencing the recent developments on demands of democratic rights by the people throughout the world it may be emphasised that "communication facility" must be for all as communication is a human need, communication is a delegated right and communication is a liberation process. Again it is proved that no longer Government or rulers are able to operate effectively, to control, censor or to play the role of gate-keeper with regard to communication net-works at all times in a given society. Both alternate and parallel net-works which may not always be active often function through political, socio-cultural, religious or class structures or can be based upon secular, cultural, artistic or folklorist channels.

The freedom of right to communicate, therefore, must be approached from a three fold perspective. First, it is necessary for the public to participate effectively in the communication field. Secondly, there is the design of a framework in which this can take place. And thirdly, the media must enjoy professional autonomy, free of economic, political or whatever pressure. And then only, development strategy will achieve its desired goal utilising the communication inputs.

3. Extension Methods and Models for Effective Extension Programmes

Extension effectiveness in transferring important agricultural technologies from research to the farmer in the most of the third world countries has been generally disappointing. As a result, many have become disillusioned with extension as a viable technology diffusion vehicle. Though, many may not agree with this observation, but to one thing every one agrees that there is an urgent need for integrating communication input in extension projects for achieving desired agricultural development objectives. The development of effective communication strategies and their integration into agricultural development projects must be the major theme for any short-term strategic agricultural development programme.

Extension Institution and programmes exist virtually in every developing country. Yet, coverage of farm families is still limited, the effectiveness of extension as a viable technology diffusion vehicle has been seriously questioned and returns on investment in extension are still not established. Considering this situation several questions are being asked, particularly, for the need and effectiveness of extension programme for achieving agricultural development objectives. Some of these questions are :

* Is extension programme actually as ineffective as it may appear to be in many countries ?
* Is there justification for continuing support and strengthening extension in its present form ?
* If not, can extension be re-oriented, re-directed,

re-designed and transformed into a more viable force for technology transfer ? And how can this be accomplished ?

* Do the root cause of disappointing extension performance lie with the extension concept ? Or have there been external factors that have limited its effectiveness ?

It is true that it will be difficult to answer all the questions as situation varies country to country with regard to technology, extension process, clients, infrastructure and support systems, but some of the common, relevant and significant indicators, for planning and implementing the effective communication support for technology transfer projects are discussed below.

The lack of rapid and consistent adoption by third world farmers of improved technologies that could increase their production and productivity demonstrates the need for extension or some other type of technology diffusion and transfer institution. Although, widespread farmer adoption may occur with minimal benefit from organised extension activity in the occasional cases of spectacular technological break-through, this does not necessarily hold true for the more common case of technologies with more modest potential returns and more limited ranges of adaptation.

Research must provide direction to and be intimately involved in the process in which the researcher can help directly in disseminating technological information to the farmers. Some farmers will learn about new technologies through serving as a co-operators for field test or observing such tests in programmes but many more will not. Some effective mechanism is needed to disseminate this information to all farmers.

Farmers need continuing assistance in learning how to apply new technologies and in coping with problems that emerge as they are used. Although, researchers can provide some such assistance, their primary job is research. Can they, again provide that assistance on the scale needed. Researchers can and should, however, provide technical support to an institution that is, direct and continuing contact with those farmers.

Farmers may also need help in finding out where and how they can obtain the goods and services. They need to take advantage of new technologies. In the situations where the agricultural infrastructure is not yet developed, such "non technological" factors must be taken into consideration. A mechanism is needed for coordinating farmers' needs and interests with recommendations and provision of needed goods and services. Thus, the *need* for extension or other technology diffusion agency is well-established.

The major problems extension are facing today in most of the developing countries as identified by development workers are :

* Conventional extension methods have relied heavily on interpersonal communication channels using the field extension agents. Even though the number of people raised this way can be increased through various mechanisms such as the "Contact Farmer" concept in the "Training and Visit" Sytsem. The number of agents is still seldom sufficient to cover an area adequately.

* Field extension agents and Subject Matter Specialists are often inadequately trained and incentives are not sufficient.

* Backstopping of extension agents in the field is deficient.

* Lack of effective co-ordination between research and extension is a common problem.

* The agricultural technologies recommended to farmers have not always been appropriate and well adapted; and in formulating them insufficient consideration has been given to farmers' attitudes, needs, desires and constraints.

* Feedback from the field to extension, research and the suppliers of goods and services needed by farmers is commonly irratic and inadequate.

* "Non-technological" constraints to adoption of new technologies are too often not given sufficient attention in planning the extension programme.

* Productivity of extension workers is often limited by lack of funds to provide majority and other operational support.

* Audio-visual aids and other various communication media have been used extensively; but their use has often meant add-on and ad-hoc in nature rather than being integrated into the total extension programme.

* Extension institution and programmes are typically bureaucratised to the point that they are permanently established and not readily amenable to represent radical change.

It is true that extension has a potential to become a viable and effective technology diffusion agency. To realise that potential, however, it will be necessary for extension to be re-oriented, re-designed and re-directed. For this purpose, new and innovative approaches to the entire technology development and transfer process will be required. The relevant question, therefore, becomes under what conditions and how can extension realise its inherent potential as an effective vehicle for technology transfer ? Of the changes needed, six major ones are identified below. The process of such change is already under way in a number of developing countries' projects and programmes.

First, extension programme must be farmer-oriented and farmer must be and feel involved.

Second, linkages and coordination between research and extension must be strengthened. On-farm testing to determine technology adaptation and farmer reactions is a key step in which joint research extension involvement is critical.

Third, well planned and appropriate multi-media communication strategies must be incorporated into the extension programme.

Fourth, coordination within the extension programme, between extension and research, and among the farmers, extension and research and the suppliers of goods and services must be given high priority. Many potentially successful programmes have not lived up to expectation due to lack of such coordination and lack of regular uninterrupted flow of information among all involved in or impacting upon the programme.

Fifth, constraints, over which extension can have no control—land, agricultural infrastructure, Government policies, etc., must be taken into consideration in determining the technical content of the extension programme. Extension can influence technology transfer only if such constraints can be alleviated, in some cases, extension may be able to contribute toward their alloviation, and

Sixth, the re-oriented, re-designed, re-directed and re-vitalised extension programmes must be institutionalised. Competent staff must be placed and maintained in position, trained and given experience during the revitalisation process that will enable them to provide capable and imaginative leadership to extension programmes in future. Government too must recognize the new roles and methods of extensi on.

Until the types of changes identified above are accepted and institutionalised, the likelihood that any important extension programme developed with external assistance will persist is not encouraging. In addition to the improvements and strengthening required to make present extension service effective technology diffusion vehicles, another potentially important force for changing needs to be incorporated in the total technology transfer system.

The private sector and other relevant public sector institutions need to be directly involved and participate fully in the technology transfer thrust. Collectively they usually have more people in the field than extension. The private sector typically has more flexibility in operation than the public sector, and it can provide additional effective channels for reaching and receiving feedback from the farmers. It may sometimes be both more effective and more cost effective to turnover to private sector agencies or to an autonomous public sector entity, a major portion of the responsibility for technology transfer. It may be true in most of the developing countries but may not be possible and effective in India. India's technology transfer effort specially in agriculture must be governed and implemented by Government agencies as it has vast areas and typical varying situational factors responsible for production and development.

At last, the need for extension or some other technology diffusion vehicle is recognised. Extension performance has been disappointing today although, the basic extension concept is valid. Improvement will depend upon the introduction and institutionalisation of new and innovative approaches to the entire technology development and transfer system. Some of the more important changes that will be required have been identified and the process of change has started. It must be accelerated and extended throughout the developing world if extension is to meet the present day challenge to become a force for technology transfer that promotes continued agricutural progress and development.

Different Extension Models for Agricultural Development

There is no extension model that is best for all countries or even for the same country at all stages in its development. To suit the country's extension infrastructure and resources availability, extension model should be drawn, modified and adapted.

In the early years of US extension, county agents worked with the local people on a wide variety of agricultural problems of which the dissemination of information about important agricultural technologies and practices was only a part. A shift to more intensive emphasis on the technology transfer came later as agricultural infrastructure and research programmes became established.

Present day US extension bears little resemblance to those early days. Farmers are well educated and have direct access to new technological information through innumerous challenge, infrastructure is well developed and other institutions including an agri-business sector, provided much of the technical infromtion and many of the services formerly required from extension.

The typical developing countries situation today resembles in some respects with United States during the early years of US extension. Even though, information dissemination is important, it is not in itself sufficient to bring about widespread technology transfer. In other respects, the typical developing country situation today is more complex, particularly, with regard to socio-economic and other cultural and political issues.

Orivel (1983) has identified three underlined philosophies of extension projects, however, that can be used as the basis for conceptualising three distinct types of extension—the first three 'models' mentioned below. A forth general model, which incorporates the types of approaches discussed in the above part of this Chapter, is then offered as an alternative more nearly relevant to the needs of today.

The models identified and discussed below are over-simplified to highlight the dominant characteristics of each. Elements of all can be found in virtually every extension programme. None is likely to fit in existing situation, exactly.

I. The "Directive" Extension Model

Extension services based on this model typically employ "top-down" methods imposed from above by politicians, planners, technocrats, and leaders who set a number of 'targets' to be achieved by the farmers. The programme is frequently administered through a series of "schemes" each of which is directed toward persuading farmers to do whatever may be required to achieve one or a set of those targets.

Farmers' participation in determining goals, objectives and what would be most desirable to meet their own needs is minimal in this model. In other word, the farmer is viewed as a passive recipient of information rather than an active participant. It is paradoxical that Benor and Harrison's "Training and Visit" system (1977), a major effort made in the '70s to revitalise agricultural extension services, embodies the most radical version of the directive system, thus far (Orivel, 1983). As pointed out by Johnston & Clarke, (1982) however, key features of the Benor approach have been creation of organizational structure and institutional procedures to provide tighter linkages between research and extension and the identification and promotion of innovations that are feasible and worthwhile at the farm level. Also the focus on selected "contact farmers" to assist in spreading new practices quickly to farmers in their communities offers potential for both obtaining a multiplying effect and the developing mechanisms for obtaining regular feedback from the farmers. Thus, it will be more appropriate to term the Training and Visit System a 'modified' directive model.

II. The "Participatory" Extension Model

No matter, how well intentioned they may be, it is unlikely

that planners and technocrats can have sufficient familiarity with the highly devised agricultural needs, constraints and potentials in every region and sub-region in the country to enable them to design national programmes appropriate for all farmers and all regions. Recognition of these programmes has lead to development of extension programmes in which farmers are viewed as participants in decision-making and implementation rather than as passive recipients.

Although some variation on the participatory model characterises most extension programmes undertaken in recent years through out the developing world, insufficient attention has been given to understanding the farmer—his attitudes, present farming enterprise, resources and other constraints, socio-cultural characieristics and economic situation. As a result although such programmes are benefited from farmers' participation, most have still not become truly farmer-oriented.

The large number of farmers, many of whom have very small holdings and live in which communication and movement are difficult, present a major problem in implementing a participatory extension approach. Direct involvement of every farmer in decisions concerning extension programme content, cope up at the sacrifice of other activities, essential to the technology development and transfer process. Compromises must be made to assure effective farmer participation without jeopardizing the technology diffusion, role of extension. Unless participation is truely representative, the problems specific to small farmers with limited resources (which is very common throughout the developing world) may not be identified.

III. The "Contractual" Extension Model

The contractual concept of extension is manifested in various forms, all of which represented a major departure from conventional public extension services in which all costs are borne by society as a whole.

As first variant, farmers contract with development/extension agency to obtain technical assistance and market outlets in return for which the farmers agree to follow the agency's instructions.

A second variant is the practice in Sri Lanka and elsewhere of permitting animal production and health extension agents to charge farmers' for their veterinary services.

In a third variant, farmers' services societies, farmers associations, cooperatives or similar organizations may employ their own extension staff to work directly with their members. In this variant, the primary public extension service point of contact with the farmers is through such organizations' extension staff.

As a modification of the contractual model concept, a Government may contract with a private sector organization to provide all extension services on its behalf. Under certain conditions, some variant of the contractual model, may be the most viable "solution" to the extension problem in terms of the effectiveness and public sector costs. The decision must be situation specific and it can not be generalised and considering India's vastness this contractual model may not be applicable everywhere in the country.

IV. The "Hybrid" Extension Model Need for Today

Elements of the models identified and discussed above need to be incorporated into a hybrid model to meet today's needs. Farmers participation, as in the participatory model, is critically important. Yet strong support and direction from above are needed to mobilise resources effectively and to achieve and maintain the degree of internal and inter-institutional coordination essential to a successful technology transfer programme.

And ways must be found to involve the private sector productively and effectively.

The structure and operational procedures of extension will vary from country to country and sometimes within a country, depending upon the extension institution, situations and opportunities. Whatever may be the from, however, extension appropriate for today and in the forseeable future needs to :

* Be farmer-oriented. Extension must understand the farmer and the farmer must be an active participant in the programme rather than a simple passive recipient of information and instruction.
* Coordinate and collaborate closely with research in identification of problems, determination of adaptation and potential farmer acceptance of new technologies.
* Collaborate with research in planning, establishing, conducting and assessing the results of on-farm trials.
* Coordinate its educational and information programmes with Government and the suppliers of goods and services to assure that for each technology recommended, the farmers will have access to require inputs, services and markets.
* Develop and maintain the effective feedback systems and communication networks to facilitate the two way flow of information between and among the farmers, research, extension, suppliers of goods and services, government and other relevant public and private sector institutions; and
* Incorporate viable communication strategies and support into the total extension programmes.

If all these strategies stated above are incorporated and systematised in all extension programmes meaningfully and effectively the achievement of development programmes objectives will be easier and less time consuming.

References

Benor, Daniel, and James Q. Harrison, 1977. Agricultural Extension; The Training and Visit System. World Bank, Washington, D.C.

Johnston, B.F., and W.C. Clark. 1982. *Redesigning Rural Development, a Strategic Perspective.* The John Hopkins University Press, Baltimore.

Orivel, Francois, 1983. The Impact of Agricultural Extension; a Review of the Literature, *Basic Education and Agricultural Extension*; *Cost, Effects and Alternatives.* World Bank Staff Working Paper Number 564. Washington, D.C.

THREE

Agricultural Development Strategy Vis-A-Vis Agricultural Extension Programmes for the Future

The broad pattern of agricultural revolution of the kind currently taking place in India and other third world countries of the world requires as its own local strategies, the extension of irrigation, much greater fertilizers use, availability of plentiful seed of high yielding varieties and above all, adequate support prices to maintain inputs at rising level dictated by new technologies. Except for new fertilizer plants, these are all, happily not capital intensive activities. This has meant what is truly decisive economic change, a great improvement in the efficiency of capital employed in the economy as a whole. Much of the shortage of capital in developing countries is to be related to the low efficiency of capital in "large scale" industry: scales of operation are not large enough to obtain the full economies of scale.

The Central sphere head of social change in the grand design to transfer our economic and social systems in the coming decades is employment. Employment has both in its human and economic components, the largest measure of thrust of any of the major strategies of economic change.

First, the volume of new employment must be related closely to the total volume of all output. There is no sense, even crude economic sense, in making output rise without a corresponding rise in employment. For in all our societies capital is scarce and labour abundant. But the particular character of the employment to be provided in the 2000 AD will determine much more specifically the nationsl success in making poor more productive. Employment has a both qualitative and quantitative dimension and the farmer is the more important for revolutionary change. It is the character of the change in the labour force, that has engineered the chain of productivity improvements which the world had seen in the last three and half centuries.

Second, the agricultural revolution first ejects excessive labour engaged in low productivity undertakings and then the prosperity produced by invention and innovation directs the unemployed persons into alternative production. The new employment whether in agro-based or new industries, creates greater wealth and therefore, commands a higher wage, inducing further improvement away from stagnant methods of production. The large chain reaction in the labour force often described in treaties on the Morphology of labour from low production and low income brackets generally in the agricultural and primary sectors, to the higher secondary sectors in the first instance and then, largely in the late 20th century revolution from the secondary to the tertiary sector on conspecuously higher salaries and at conspecuously novel and specificated occupations. The constant revolution in technology which has taken the place of the fitful and occasional inventions which first unloosed the agricultural and industrial revolutions in the modern world has kept the tempo of change continous.

The central force of change being employment, it is essential to plan, not by the operations of chance, but by a design the volume of employment which each sector is to provide for the next decade and beyond. In the revolution design to make the poor more productive, obviously, there must be a deliberate choice in favour of the high income occupations against those at the lower end of the spectrum. This implies that agriculture will be consistently deprived of its excessive labour force and that tertiary occupation will be developed much more rapidly than has been the case over the last 30 years or so.

The character of the strategies required for rapid economic and social change must be set in what might be described as the cultural grooves appropriate for local involvement and hard but congenial work. The supplies of missing ingradients, by whatever agencies of capital and technology help, but they do not, when massively injected, always, or even generally get massively absorbed. It is in the rapid observation of productive capital in the social milieu, in which the people have already made their occupational choice that the secret of rapid economic development resides. This is in fact the major element in reducing the capital : output ratio in the short period. If the projects fit into an existing cultural patten, the original capital injected spreads rapidly recipients and among the 'natural' ancillaries which are by-products of the original recipients. There is currently at work in the Indian Union an efficient protoype of an economic and social revolution of just this type.

Hence, a new directive, a new thinking, and a new approach are necessary today to exploit and utilise the knowledge and experiences of the farmers and development workers and to learn the lessons from positive outcome of several extension and other development programmes with participatory communication for meeting the future challenges in agriculture in the Third World and other developing countries.

Keeping this in mind the present Chapter has been designed to highlight various facets of agricultural development strategy and extension programmes for the future in three different heads ;

1. Agricultural Extension Programmes – present and future;
2. Indigenous Knowledge Use in Agriculture; and
3. Participatory Communication for Development Actions in Agriculture.

1. Agricultural Extension Progammes—Present and Future

It is almost four decades now that agricultural extension programme has been officially launched in India (since introduction of Community Development Programme in 1952.) Basically the model and the content of the Official Extension Programme was adopted from USA. Accordingly, the support system for the extension programme in terms of institutions, training programmes, services and supply mechanisms and organisations have been built over the years in ever expanding rate. However, there is hardly any significant change in the model and content of the original extension programme except in minor variation in emphasis such as present Danial Benor's Training and Visit System (T & V) of Extension. But with the present change of society, people's expectations, availability of modern technology and high competition in agricultural production systems among the countries of the world, it is high time to critically review the agricultural extension systems of our country in order to develop a programme relevant for the country's situation. Looking back historically, one really wonders about the contribution of Agricultural Extension Programme in the progress achieved in India's agricultural development and alleviation of rural poverty. The extension programme must change its approach and system to cope up with the drastic change occured recently in the overall dynamics of rural India, to achieve its success. But before analysing the required change in the system, it would be worthwhile to examine the existing system.

Essentially the extension programme in the existing system is an agent for transferring the technical knowledge and skill and services between a fairly organised "delivery system" and a largely unorganised "receiving system." In other words, the extension system is inter-face linkage between delivery system and the receiving system.

The delivery system as it developed over the years, has been an organised system and that too largely in a bureaucratic framework. The output of the delivery system, therefore, follows the norms and interest of a highly skilled manpower empowered with its organizational strengths and weaknesses. On the other hand, the receiving system has remained basically unorganised characterised by large numbers widely dispersed in the rural areas and widely heterogenious interest groups. And as a result the existing agricultural extension system could not achieve its desired objectives or could not make much headway to combat the farmers' problems.

This is not to highlight or suggest that the delivery system is unproductive and totally ineffective. Neither it is implied here that technology and capital, which the delivery system is designed to provide for the receiving system are not essential for development and extension programme. Whether large or small farmers or landless labourers, technology and capital are crucially required and wanted by all. What is suggested here is the fact that so long as the interface between two systems is not strengthened by organising the receiving system at a comparable level, the process of transfer of output of the 'delivery' system through the extension agents will remain incomplete, partial and ineffective for a large part of the poor peasants.

The big question comes, then what needs to be done ? The aforesaid analysis clearly indicates the absolute necessity for organising the "receiving" system in close consonance with the delivery system. It is to be understood very clearly that the leakages and ineffectiveness of the transfer mechanism through the extension system is largely due to the weak interface resulting from imbalances and incompatibilities between the delivery and receiving systems. Therefore, the priorities of roles and functions of the agricultural extension system need to be re-oriented and re-designed.

Need for Alternative Approach to Agricultural Extension System

The imbalances between the delivery and receiving systems can be corrected largely by concentrating the efforts in organising the rural population that is the receiving system. The rural population truly the rural poor can be meaningfully and effectively organised atleast to start with around an activity which benefits them economically and in which the beneficiaries' perceived risk is the bare minimum. This means, the services and technical output of the delivery system should have to be transferred by the extension agents to the receiving rural population without leakages and distortion in the process and then the process needs to be sustained over a period of time until such time the process becomes internalized by the groups of receivers who develop their own capabilities and competencies to maintain and monitor the flow.

It is doubtful whether such a complete shift in the roles of existing extension system is possible within the bureaucratic framework. Having said that, let us try to explain the alternative roles of the extension system. Take for example, the role of transferring information is one of the basic functions of the existing extension system. The fundamental hypothesis behind this role is the fact that the transfer of technology and capital can be effective only when the receivers understand, defend and enforce the delivery system in the form of development programmes and institutions owning or providing the technology and capital. For this to be the reality, the receiving system must be informed. And it is the transfer of information which has the potential seed to start the process of organising the receiving system effectively.

Like this the possibilities or potentialities are enormous to revamp the agricultural extension system, but equally those are time consuming. What it needs is a different orientation and priorities for the agricultural extension programme. It calls for a serious re-orientation of the existing extension training/ education and research programme. Re-orientation may look unpalatable and dangerous to those who have developed vested interest in the exising system. But failing re-orientation, the consequences are sure to be disastrous. The choices to the extension specialists and policy makers therefore is between unpalatable and disaster.

Alternative Approach

From the experiences of last four decades of various extension programmes, extension developments in India and visualising likely demand to be placed in this regard in 2000 AD, we may draw some important lessons for future extension strategy for the development in agriculture and its alternative approach to accomplish desired objectives.

Firstly, the extension has to rely more and more upon research and it can no longer be a mere passive recipient of technology from the research. The extension has to become active and should demand appropriate technology from research.

Secondly, the farmers' problems must be communicated to research more effectively and practical solutions are to be obtained. Extension must establish a two-way linkage of research, within research-extension-farmer, and farmer extension-research.

Third and lastly, the community of agricultural scientists must be exposed to the discipline of extension to enable them design appropriate technological packages for their cilents—the farmers. Considering these how well we go about it, will be a challenge to our management capability of extension and other development programmes in the coming years.

Further, there is explicit emphasis today througnout the world on professionalism in extension. This shows that the requirements of 2000 AD can be met only by a professional extension services. This also shows that amateur approaches characteristic of an amateur extension worker lie firmly burried in the 1980s. Basically, the definition of extension characterises that it is an educational process. As such a pronounced emphasis is required to ensure that the technology oriented extension does not lose the sight of its primary educational function. It also retains induction of behavioural changes in the farmers. This is very much essential and pre-requisite for the adjustment of farmers to their changed socio-cultural and politico-economic environment. The present day 'extension' should have also clear emphasis on increased income which is the end result of extension. This is the ultimate test for the success of extension.

The future definition of extension makes the role of communication in extension explicit. But the role of communication means proven methods of communication i.e., technological information must reach to the users and it is adapted in practice and desired outcome achieved as expected.

Lastly, the definition of extension lays stress on diffusion—adoptation of innovations. It is not the case of extension that there can not be any diffusion adoption of agricultural innovations without extension. Infact, for centuries and for ages diffusion adoption has taken place without extension and would continue to take place without extension. The case of extension today is that extension can speed up the process of diffusion adoption of innovations. It is this speed which will and does determine the rate of agricultural development.

Therefore, today extension as a strategy for Transfer of Technology, change and development has gained world-wide acceptability. Many countries in the world have introduced country-wide officially sponsored national agricultural and extension systems. In India, we perhaps require the same if we want to make dent into the present agricultural production and productivity scenario.

India once again face the challenge of increased agricultural production and productivity as it enters 1990s. It has built up necessary competence characterised by its agricultural scientists, extension personnel and appropriate infrastructure to face the challenge of 1990s with confidence, resilience and maturity. Agricultural extension will play an important role in facing the challenges of agricultural production and productivity in 2000 AD and well beyond if we suitably redesign and remodel our extension approach for the purpose and also make sure the people's involvement in our all extension programmes.

Peoples' Involvement in Extension Programmes

Community involvement is one of the basic requirements of community development. There is a great deal of empirical evidence to support this justification, and it cannot be denied that direct handling of large scale projects of commnnity development particularly, the agricultural aspect by the administration is costly and unproductive. The denial of participation of the people in vital decision-making process withholds from them the educative experience which alone can prepare them for effective self-help. It is suggested, therefore, that planning and execution responsibility of agricultural extension programmes under community development may ideally shift from administration to the people through three stages from *planning for the people* to *planning with the people* and then on to *planning by the people*.

This is very much important and significant when agricultural innovations are adopted by the farmers for increasing their farm productivity and income. The first two stages must necessarily be brief, even in the first stage, the people should be associated as much as possible with every aspect of planning and implementation. This can be done either by creating series of new institutions to discharge fundamental functions, or by involving the extension institutions of local governments in these responsibilities. To avoid duplication involved in two parallel stages of institutions, many countries have chosen the path of remodelling local government to adapt it for the tasks of development.

It is in the attainment of the objective of development of people's initiative, their competence, and their resources through their own institutions that the community development so far has failed to make its mark. Various evaluation reports and research studies reveal that people's reaction in most of the development blocks of the country are not yet generally favourable for the growth and self-reliance in village community development programmes. The majority of the villagers do not record it as their own and seem to rely mainly on the Government for effecting the development of the rural areas. The basic philosophy and approach of community development programmes are therefore, inadequately subscribed to by the people in these areas.

The achievement of community development through agricultural extension programmes so far in this country has been of cummunity development assets, the question only the creation then faces us is whether that was the most efficient method of creation of these assets? The adequacy or other ways of production of these assets is a matter purely circumscribed by the amount of finance made available to the programme. People become happy in receiving some material benefits or financial benefits which ultimately do not help them. Peoples' programme, therefore, must be planned, designed and implemented with the participation of the people actively. Then only, desired outcome or successful attainment of objectives takes place.

Role of Social Science Research in Agricultural Development

Community development cannot be a progressive process without the support of research and the guidance of evaluation. And important aspect of community development covers the extension of modern science and technology to the under developed societies. This is a two way process. If under developed societies have to adapt themselves to science and technology, in turn, the science and technology will also have to adapt themselves to the conditions of under developed societies. In this area research has an important function. It must find answers to local contexts. A network of scientific organizations geared to this purpose thus becomes necessary. It should cover a wide spectrum of activities—agriculture and animal husbandry, rural industries and engineering, sanitation and public health and many more cognet areas of action.

The function of social research in this context is not less important. As an aid to planning and development it should provide :

1. background studies for realistic policy making;
2. analysis of emerging trends and patterns; and
3. Diagnostic studies of problem areas, where obstinate resistance to planned change is met.

Again, research and evaluation can not be separated. In fact, evaluation is research of a special type. Unless, the evaluation of a programme is done, we can not cope up with the changing scenario of the problem and the plan of action will not carry really needed solution to that problem. Therefore, the evaluation should be on going and continuous. And it should be aimed at :

1. Measuring in both quantitative and qualitative terms, the degree of success with which plans are impelmented and changes are introduced;

2. Identifying drifts and difficulties as well as pitfalls and bottlenecks;
3. Locating unanticipated consequences promoted innovations; and
4. Exploring the tangibles and intangibles and imponderables governing the acceptance or rejection of changes in all aspects.

Developmental agencies are nearly always in hurry. That accept partly their insistence of quick applied research. And artificial distinction is often made between fundamental and applied research, without realising that a backlog of good fundamental research, is a pre-requisite to analyses of an applied nature. In both research and evaluation, the emphasis is on hurried surveys that often touch only the surface. Their design leaves much to be desired, and the manner in which they are conducted—mostly by functionaries of Government having real orientation to research—does not inspire confidence in the reliability and validity of the findings. There is little evidence to suggest that Governments are cognisant of the need of long-term research and evaluation in depth.

The hard fact remains that the social science have not given of their best to research having a bearing, direct or indirect, on community development. At the same time one may wonder how research findings, such as they exist have been used in policy making and programme planning. Research is fashionable these days and most development organizations do have research wings and institutes of their own. But channels for effective utilisation of research findings will remain to be explored. The social scientist must therefore, cast aside some of their traditional aloofness and the politician and the administrator should start exploring the deeper import of research and evaluation. Even good developmental programmes could be made better by purposeful organization of research and evaluation and by their meaningful utilisation.

New Thrust to Extension Programme Through Community Development

Community Development is a process. To produce lasting results, it must continue for a fair length of time. The priorities of community development should be on agricultural production and productivity. The programmes should be in such a way phased that there are built in pauses for stock taking. This should provide the time for critical heart-searching and for taking integrated view of the total achievements and of the sum of the evaluations and assessments. Major policy changes should be decided at this stage. Some important questions to be considered at this stage are :

1. Is it necessary to redefine the focus and priorities ?
2. Do extension methods need any modification ?
3. What successful experience can be extended elsewhere and how ?
4. What projects and methods must be written off as having been tried but as having failed ?

The timing of such stock-taking is of crucial significance. It must not be done on quick intervals; results of a series of inter-related projects should be allowed to stabilize themselves to permit an integrated view of achievements and failure. The tendency towards morbid heart-searching at too frequent intervals and towards quick policy changes must be guarded against. Community development especially in its institution building aspect is a slow process and impatience to active results can be a major factor tn its failure. Therefore, in the redesigned and renewed efforts to provide a popular base to community devlopment and effective agricultural extension programme through decentralisation of government power and involvement of people, one should read signs of hope.

2. Indigenous Knowledge Use in Agriculture

In the 1930s crop yields in the United States, England, India and Argentina were essentially the same. In some areas of the world, yield increases since than have been modest. However, other parts of the world have witnessed dramatic yield increases. This success has not been without social cost. And today, throughout the world, the concept of "Alternative Agriculture" is being stressed for higher productivity by utilising local available resources. "The hall-mark of an alternative farming approach is not the conventional practices which rejects, but the practices which includes—alternative systems more deliberately integrate and take advantage of naturally occuring beneficial interactions."

As a society, we have, at times made serious mistakes by trying to transplant technology developed in one culture, under one economic system and suited to one set of climatic and soil variables into a Thrid World country where these factors were totally different. In the process, traditional methods of production that represented the wisdom of many generations were ignored. And as new technology is adopted throughout the world, traditional knowledge is in danger of being lost when those who possess it grow old.

To develop the methodologies for recording, documenting, and preserving the traditional practices of the indigenous farmer, Centre for Indigenous Knowledge in Agriculture and Rural Development (CIKARD), in Iowa State University, USA was established in 1987.

This traditional knowledge in agricultural operation is used to guide agricultural scientists as they develop and disseminate management practices. This process integrates the understanding of nature and agriculture, based on generations of experience of local farmers with latest scientific understanding.

Today, it is widely accepted among the agricultural scientists throughout the world that for introducing new agricultural technology, the reassessment of indigenous technical knowledge of agriculture is a must. There is no two opinion that farmers have a wealth of knowledge of their own environment and have developed specific skills to use this environment. Therefore, it is of utmost importance that farmers' knowledge are taken into account before any agricultural technology is developed and disseminated to its users.

Indigenous Knowledge (IK)

According to Warren (1989), "Indigenous knowledge is local knowledge—knowledge that is unique to a given culture or society. This knowledge is the information base for a society, codified in the language of the society, it facilitates communication and decision making. Indigenous knowledge is dynamic which changes through indigenous creativity and innovativeness as well as through contact with other knowledge systems."

Each society has a variety of types of knowledge systems; some deal with the natural and physical environment, some with the cognitive and ideational (value systems) environment and others with the social environment. Indigenous knowledge is passed down through generation to generation, usually by word-of-mouth. Indigenous knowledge systems often are elaborate and they are adapted to local, cultural and environmental conditions. Development professionals through out the world increasingly are seeing the value of this type of knowledge in solving agricultural and environmental problems.

Recognition of farmers' knowledge and innovative capacity does not necessarily mean that they do not need extension services. Rather, it points to needs to improve the interaction between extensionists and farmers to reverse and balance conventional 'top-down' communication and to overcome gaps and distorted communication.

The knowledge, skills and survival strategies of farmers operating with low levels of external inputs have often been ignored or even eroded by outsiders promoting "modern" agricultural technology. However, with increasing awareness of the limitations and hazards of conventional agriculture, a growing number of scientists have begun to recognise indigenous knowledge as a major untapped resource for developing sustainable agriculture. Local practices offer joining points for developing ways of increasing the productivity and sustainability of local resources. Indigenous knowledge can reveal missing ecological keys which may help scientists develop alternative agricultural technologies less dependent on non-renewable resources (eg., fossil energy) and environmentally damaging inputs (eg., chemical pesticides) than conventional technologies.

Traditional Agriculture and Agricultural Development

Traditional agriculture, can make important contributions to agricultural research, help conservation biological diversity, and maintain healthy relations between rural people and the land. For example, a wide range of crops, even over 100 at one time can be grown in traditional systems of shifting (Jhum) cultivation, essentially transformation of natural forest into a harvestable land. Although, Swidden agriculture has come under wide abuse as being destructive of forests and watersheds, it is highly adaptive to a wide range of conditions and when properly performed, it is the only sustainable way of cultivating the areas where poor soils, steep gradients and healthy rainfall make conventional farming methods unproductive or impossible. As practised by stable groups, Swidden agriculture is not particularly destructive of forests, land or wild life. Permanent villages are established, moving only if forced to do so by extremes of economic hardships, political disturbances or population pressure, not as logical consequences of their agricultural techniques (Hinton 1970).

The challenge is to find ways of enabling the traditional agricultural research systems—such as shifting cultivation to contribute for evolving relationships between people and their living resources. Traditional agriculture has adapted to wide variety of local environments, producing diversity and reliability of food supply, reducing instance of disease and insect problems, using labour efficiently intensifying production with limited resources and earning maximum returns under low levels of technology.

This traditional agriculture utilises a very wide variety of species and land-races which vary in their reaction to disease and insect pests, and to different conditions of soil, rainfall and temperature. It provides sustainable yields by drawing on centuries of accumulated experience by farmers who did not depend on scientific information, external inputs, capital, credit or markets.

Higher Productivity from Traditional Agriculture

With the advent of growing population throughout the world, steps need to be taken to enhance the productivity of land under traditional agriculture. In this regard, indigenous knowledge of the farmers is most important by which agricultural productivity can be enhanced under traditional farming practices. In up-lands, modern agricultural development should take existing Swidden systems as starting point and use modern agricultural science to improve on the productivity of the system. Development should be based on the ability of the Swidden farmers to adapt to change but would continue to draw on resources conserving and yield sustaining production technology (Altieri and Merrick, 1987). The essential element is the design of self-sustaining agro-ecosystems which assure the maintenance of local genetic diversity available to farmers, thereby enabling rural communities of Swidden cultivators to maintain control over their production systems.

In addition, the ability to maintain a stable and permanent relationship with forest land enables some Swidden farmers to invest time and effort in other permanent assets like fruit trees, fenced gardens, terraces, and irrigation channels. In the most suitable areas, tne Swiddens are supplemented by irrigated rice-fields, thus allowing a considerably higher population density than under Swidden conditions alone. Such mixed systems will often enable modern agricultural techniques to be wedded to the traditional ones, and lead to the establishment of more permanent villages and subtainable agriculture.

Agricultural Research and Rural Poor

Large areas of forest which are protected against outside encroachment and assigned to specific ethnic groups for sustainable management might be a means of ensuring the productivity of shifting cultivation systems, coupled with a research effort aimed at ensuring a steady delivery of contributions to agricultural development. In some places, community-level "landrace custodians" could be given subsidies, if necessary, to maintain their traditional agricultural systems which enable the continuing evolution of genetic diversity important to agricultural development.

Research aimed at benefitting the poorest farmers should be based on the ecological approach and on existing traditional agriculture. This might include the development of more efficient low-input agricultural systems based on biological recycling of energy and chemical nutrients, and relying primarily on naturally occuring control mechanisms for crop protection. It should seek to develop new agricultural systems, often building on rediscovered or newly appreciated traditional systems. A wide spectrum of agricultural crops should be considered, including many which might be viewed as "non-traditional." Restoring, maintaining and improving the natural resource base should be the basis for offering farmers a reasonable chance for economic betterment.

Need for Development Wisdom

Agricultural ecologists have learned to respect the wisdom inherent in much traditional practice. Involving the ultimate clients of agricultural research in both the design and testing of improved technology will allow specialists to capture some of the practical knowledge about agro-ecosystems, and offer greater assurance that new methods will be more widely adopted once their effectiveness has been demonstrated. Within its limits, traditional farming can continue to make a meaningful input into the total agricultural productivity of the regional and contribute to the biological diversity of the tropical forest eco-system, if it is developed as part of the overall system of conservation-oriented management. This blending of traditional agriculture with modern agricultural technologies is very much important for sustainable growth and development in Agriculture in Third World nations.

3. Participatory Communication for Development Action in Agriculture

Participatory Communication is the main theme of development communication. Participatory Message Construction must focus or highlight on the grass root problems and needs of the intended clientele in development process, particularly, in agriculture and rural development programmes. This approach leads to reduce knowledge gaps and increase self-reliance of the intended receivers. Therefore, involvement of the intended receivers is required and enables use of their indigenous knowledge. Ideally people who are affected by the development programmes should have a say in their design and implementation. This should lead to greater response to development programmes where people have been involved at all the steps of the process such as identification of the problems, planning, finding possible solutions and drawing up programmes which are intended to solve specific problems. This kind of participation implies the need to involve the grass root people in constructing messages relating to such problems and programmes. This is strong justification for the need to operationalise the conceptual model of participatory message development. Also there is need to find out development communication research methodology to have greater canvas to cover all aspects of development communication.

Participation in Communication

Participatory communication is one aspect of new development paradigm. Participation may become the main theme for displacing traditional modernization theory. The modernization theory states that all the development societies still follow the same path of modernization as the western societies have followed. In this regard, Servaes (1986) noted that "since the Passing modernization paradigm developmet priorities had shifted from economic growth through capital intensive industrialization to the basic needs approach and improved quality of life for the rural people utilising their local resources. Alternatively, the post-modernization era might more optly be characterised broadly as "multiplicity in one world" and era in which societies were expected to set their own normative goals and standards which may or may not coincide with those of the post industrial west."

Further, Rogers (1976), predicted the demise of modernization's approach to communication in his article, "The Passing of the Dominant Paradigm". In it he stated that the changh agents should in the future act not as "experts" who had all the answers but instead as "resources" avilable to local people when they needed help. He noted that rather than expert predicts, *resources and change agents themselves are participants in social change.*

It is only recently that communication has become reorganized as a tool for development, i.e, communication process itself brings about a change in the communication skills of the people at the grass roots. This is a relatively new concept, perhaps coming about as a result of development studies now being recognized as an important arena for academic enquiry.

The dominant paradigm approach was mainly a "top to down", "Govt to People" communication. Information flow down from the people who thought they had the answers and may justify as to what was best was best for the people and how they had to "develop" or accept "new technologies. "Big madia" was the communication tool for creating "climates of acceptance" for solution of the peasants' problems. Solutions often were selected by foreigners and were imposed by the Government. There was no room for the peasant to be involved in the process other than to complain about what was being done to them as "beneficiaries" of development programmes.

As the new variable "participation" becomes a part of the "development equation" a need arises to reorder priorities and find ways to operationalise the concept through new communication message strategies.

Emerging Dimensions of Participation

It was during the 2nd Conference on Communication and Change at the East-West Centre in Hawaii in 1987, Development Communication scholars again became aware that there had been few peasant inputs for which decision making and that "self-determination" had been overlooked. It was their vision that perhaps, the birth of a new era of participation decision making could restore to the peasants, their right to be involved in determining their own destinies.

Soon after a new School of Development called "Another Development" emerged. They noted that the important characteristics of another development was emphasized on the need to satisfy basic human needs. They also discussed new communication perspectives which emphasized the rural communication could take involving people in the process of deciding the kind of development they wanted and what directions development might take.

The goal on participatory communication is therefore, to enable the intended receivers to take control of their own lives by providing relevant information.

Participation is seen by many persons in development including Nair & White (1987), as a process of enabling or empowering rural people to manage their own development. They noted that :

> "people must be able to educate themselves through developing thinking, acting, and problem solving abilities. Participation will give individuals a sense of power which will increase their control over the environment and free them to shape their own destiny."

Participation in its most developed form is "self management." This principle implies the right to participate in the planning and production of media content. Even more important is that intended receivers are given an opportunity to participate in decision making regarding the topics and issues of the messages.

The framework as devised by Cohen & Uphoff (1980) delineates three dimensions of participation : *What* kinds of participation can take place, *who* participates in them, and *how* the process of participation takes place.

The first dimension—*what*—is the basic one to distinguish, since participation in decision making can be different from participation in implementation. For most project designers and evaluators, the second dimension i.e., *who* may be most silent, since this deals with intended beneficiaries or receivers, whose participation is to be provided for. The third i.e., *how* adds qualitative dimension to participation, one which may be often difficult to ascertain, but which remains important for purpose of diagnosis or evaluation.

What kinds of conditions are relevant in a given situation will depend of course, on certain other factors such as projects, tasks and environment, for instance, participation in decision making, implementation, benefits and evaluation.

Participation in decision making and implementation pertains to the "inputs" of rural development projects providing authority, information, labour and other resources while people's involvement in benefit and evaluation of development activity concerns "output."

Putting people first in development projects comes down to tailoring the design and implementation of projects to the needs and capabilities of people who are proposed to benefit from them. However, according to Cohen & Uphoff (1980) no longer should people be identified as "target groups." Rather if we must speak of them abstractly we should consider them as "intended beneficiaries." They are to be "benefited" rather "impacted." In design and implementation we have only intentions since our knowledge of how to improve the productivity and well being of the poor majority is *limited*. We can and should be clear about *whom* we expect to benefit, and *how*, but we can not be certain that our efforts will bear the desired fruits until the process of economic and social change have been put in motion.

Critical *Ingredients* to participation are: participation in decision making, participation in implementation including resource mobilization, participation in benefit sharing. and participation in evaluation.

Research and Education Process in Participatory Communication

The whole research process is educational and democratic for the researcher as well as the people involved. The researcher

/hile imparting knowledge, sceks to gain knowledge through research. It is observed that when people participate actively in planning and decision activities through dialogue and discussion, the research process becomes an educational process for the people raising from critical awareness and at the same time mobilising human resources to solve problems.

An important element of participatory research is the joint analysis to be performed by the people as well as the researcher. The spirit of teamwork among the researchers and the people is also essential to facilitate participation. During the process of research, the researcher must develop his/her own analysis of reality just as the people have their own subjectively decided reality. These two are then brought into active interaction whereby a joint analysis of reality develops. The researcher can avoid pitfalls and be able to facilitate participation if he/she can successfully engage in this process of joint analysis.

(*a*) *Researcher as a facilitator*

The position of the researcher is vulnerable when he/she begins the research. There is always risk as to whether he/she will be able to successfully operationalise the theory in the real life situation. The researcher is aware of the fact that the research process requires commitment on his/her part as well as as he/she should have the ability to spend many hours in the field.

The implication, the researcher is to conduct the research using qualitative methodology and naturalistic enquiry. The researcher must conduct the research in such a way so as not to affect the natural behaviour and day to day lives of the local people. He or she should study the intended receivers naturally and over a period of time, until he gets sufficient data from his or her observation. The research design also should progress from the observations and feedback.

The role of researcher throughout the process should be that of a facilitator. One o the paradox of motivating the participation is that promoting bottom up development often requires more top-down effort. This is necessary as research progress when working with the rural people in both research settings and in order to build up organizational capacities among them. In orther words, the rural people often lack appropriate guidelines on how to identify and articulate their development questions and how to mobilising the resources. Thus, the important role of the researcher as a facilitator is to provide guidelines to facilitate participation throughout the research process rather than operating only in a top-down manner.

(*b*) *Researcher as a Development Communicator*

It is interesting to observe that low income groups rely more on interpersonal channels than on any others. These include kinship groups, friends, peer groups and opinion leaders.

The successful researcher, when involved in qualitative research must have excellent interpersonal communication skills.

This is a great asset when working with farmers. The researcher therefore, uses the interpersonal channels for development of messages to attain credibility. Interpersonal channels promote active involvement of the people in the process of developing their own communication message. While groups of people can obtain information from impersonal sources like radio and television this information is relatively ineffective in producing behavioural changes. And development communicators in the past have envisioned precisely such behavioural changes.

In this regard, the study conducted by Patel (1990) reveals that once the development communicator has worked with an intervening force i.e. a researcher or external consultant, in the process of developing participatory messages, two findings emerged :

1. The development communicator will gain confidence and the expertise to operate similarly in developing

participatory message in the future. The need for the intervening factor goes down and the development communicator will be able to predict how much and when intervention or external help will be needed.

2. The development communicator will learn the process of research. Thus role shifting takes place and the development communicator does not need to rely on constant help from the researcher. The credibility of the development communicator also increases when the messages brings successful results for the intended receivers.

Finally, to conclude the above analysis and discussion on the process of research in development communication, it may be stated that this participatory message construction involves a complex intermingling of the theory and practice of the researcher and the local people. Mutual intermingling of the theory and application must be carefully structured to a bridge rather than widen the social division between researcher/facilitator and the local people.

Another obvious implication is that there needs to be rethinking about role of the development communicator and redefinition within the roles for carrying out effective and meaningful development communication research. These development communicators have to operate at different levels of complexity of the social systems and this need varying competency levels. Role impact will be greatest in interpersonal communication competencies of development communicator. Their effectiveness will require not only specific media skills but more importantly skills which facilitate the development of people to enable them to become an integral part of the message development process. These changes do not represent an idealistic desire but an absolute necessity for development of the grass root persons' potential is truely facilitated.

References

Altieri, M.A. and Laura C. Merrick, (1987). In Situ Conservation of Crop Genetic Resources Through Maintenance of Traditional Farming Systems. *Economic Botany*, 41(1), 86-96.

Cohen, J.M. and Uphoff, N.T. (1980). "Participation's Place in Rural Development : Seeking Clarity through Specificity," *World Development*, Vol. 8, p. 213-233. Pergamon Press : London.

Hinton, P. (1970), "Swidden Cultivation among Pwo Karen of Northern Thailand" in : Proceedings of International Seminar on Shifting Cultivation and Economic Development in Northern Thailand, Land Development Department, Bangkok, pp. 1-24.

Nair, K.S. and White, Shirley A. (1987). "Participation is Key to Development Communication," *Media Development*, No. 3.

Patel, P.K. (1990). "Operationalising a Participatory Message Development Model : An Exploratory Study Using Video in a Development Context, "unpublished M.P.S. dissertation, USA, Cornell University.

Rogers, Everett M. (1976). "Communication and Development : The Passing of the Dominant Paradigm," *Communication Research*, Vol. 3, No. 2, pp. 121-133.

Servaes, Jan. (1986). "Communication and Development Paradigms : An overview," *Media Asia*, Vol. 13, No. 3, pp. 128-136.

Topel, D. and John Pesek, (1989). Indigenous Knowledge and Alternative Agriculture, *Cikard News*, 1 (4) Ames, Iowa State University.

Warren, D.M. (1989). "In-dije-nes knowledge: A Definition." *Cikard News*, 1 (1), Ames, Iowa State University.

FOUR

Community Development Strategy and Sociological Perspective of Agricultural and Rural Development

'Community Development Programme' which was launched in our country in the year 1952 represents on approach to planned change with a sense to evoke, stimulate and activate in the people of under developed areas and urge to attain increasingly higher standard of living. By and large, it is intended to be a self-help programme, but it does not rule out limited, active participation of Governmental agencies in supporting peoples' initiative and augmenting their resources. Although, its over-enthusiastic and imotional exponents have invested a mistique in the concept, community development should be viewed primarily as an approach and as a process. It is essentially a pragmatic and practical approach to multi-faceted and multi-dimensional change underlying which, there are certain fundamental assumptions that distinguish and set it apart from other approaches.

First, the community development approach visualises a sector of planning and development which could largely be left to the initiative of the people themselves. The grass root planning, desired under such programme should leave the people free to assess their needs, determine their priorities and outline their strategies of action. It is assumed that people understand their local needs best and that, given the opportunity to work for meeting their felt needs, they will in time give a good account of themselves.

Second, it is assumed that positive result can be achieved by the mobilization and utilization of the local resources—physical and human. Not many Governments, have the resources to operate directly large scale programmes of economic development and technologicol change over their entire territories. Decentralisation of the development programme and earmarking of specific areas to be developed largely through local resources can ensure wider coverage as well as reduction of costs.

Third, community development is viewed as an integrated process. Changes introduced in one area of culture tend to ramify into other areas; their consequences may be desirable and predictable in the area in which they are introduced, but they may not be so in other areas. Therefore, a comprehensive and integrated view of planning is necessary. Balanced measures of change should be introduced simultaneously in the different aspects of a community's life. The community development approach believes in working simultaneously on the economic, the social and the psychological frontiers of a community.

Fourth, it is contemplated that the entire community rather than particular individuals or particular groups in it would be brought into the focus of the development programmes. An organic view of thc community and its problems bars any possibility of orienting the programmes exclusively to specific groups. Pressing needs of a particular group should be attended to, but the community context of these needs should never be lost sight of.

Fifth, the community development is assumed to be a programme of active participation. It seeks to stimulate and activate entire community with a view to sparing its involvement in programmes of development. A community energised into activity can be expected to work for its betterment progressively. Of course, community development does not rule out the participation of a Governmental agencies; their partnership is in fact assumed. It is realised that agencies from outside the community have a vital contribution to make to its developmental process but the roles of these agencies are limited to that of catalystic agents. They are there to inform, to inspire and to stimulate, but they must not impose their priorities and emphasis on the people. The outside development agent will doubtless bring to the client community a fund of technical knowledge, the requisite human skills of community organisation, and the vision of the future. The central purpose of community development will be lost if initiative is allowed to pass from the people to outsider.

And finally, community development is to be regarded as an ongoing process. Ideally, it should progressively build the capacity of a community to absorb increasingly higher doses of modern science and technology, thereby enabling its people to improve their standards of living. As communities continue to progress, their needs inevitably continue to change. This would necessitate a shift in the targets and priorities of community development programmes. Therefore, plans are to be changed, emphasis are to be redirected, and strategies are to be redesigned as per felt needs, aspirations, resources and capability of the people.

Not only strategies of community development are important for bringing about all round development in the rural people, but also the technology which is required for increasing agricultural productivity and the extension approach which makes technology diffusion and adoption meaningful are also to be channalised in a desired direction.

Keeping all these in view, the present Chapter has been designed to discuss the different aspects of community development strategy and sociological perspective of agricultural and rural development in detail on the following three heads :

1. The Contexts of Community Development;
2. Sociological Perspective of Technology Generation in Agriculture; and
3. Extension Approach in Rural Development.

1. The Contexts of Community Development

Community development wears many masks and speaks many tongues. The complexion of a programme is determined largely by the cultural, economic, political, and admimistrative contexts in which it operates. Its language is significantly influenced by the idiom of politics and by the vocabulary of ideology. Differences in the cultural setting and the political climate inevitably colour the nature and the content as well as the emphases and the priorities of these programmes. Their adaptation to the social and the political milieu is an imperative necessity; they cannot be transferred easily from one soil to another. The economic situation sets the parameters of action and delimits the intensity and the range of development programmes; unlimited utopias cannot be pursued because most developing societies do not have the financial resources to support them. And the established administrative pattern, too, is not any less important. In many of these societies the bureaucracy functions as the prime mover for modernization and development; it can both stimulate and retard the rate of change. Thus, community development does not denote any pre-determined plan of action; on the contrary, it implies a dynamic and a variable strategy. Community development programmes in different settings, therefore, need not be identical in form; it will be enough if they preserve the essence of the approach and do not lose sight of the basic objectives.

The Cultural Context

In considering the cultural context of community devolopment, it is necessary to take account of three basic elements of the society; its structural base, its ideology, and its value orientations.

First, the developing societies have an "ascribed" status system : i.e., in them a person is born into a more or less rigidly defined status. Second, relationships in these societies tend to be of a personalised order. In other words, these societies are "particularistic" rather than "universalistic." Third, their systems of expectation and obligation are characterized by "diffuseness" rather than by "specificity." By and large, such a delineation represents the situation accurately enough but it is necessary, at the same time, to take into account the cultural complexity and the transitional nature of these societies. Alongside the masses, who largely correspond to such a description, these societies have small but significant pockets of those who are modernized, and a fairly sizeable group of those who have not yet made up their minds regarding the choice between tradition and mordernity but who have nevertheless taken some unmistakable steps in the direction of modernization. These modernized and modern izing elements cannot be ignored, because in some important aspects they contitute the "reference groups" of the masses; their significance as trend-setters and pace-setters is out of all proportion to their numerical strength. The same holds true in respect of two other major attributes of developing societies—their kin-orientation and their religious emphases. While traditional forms survive, the dents caused in them by socio-economic compulsions are meaningful.

A closer scrutiny of the structural base of developing societies appears to be indicated. It should take account of the existing plurality of the cultural ethos in these communities, and it should examine as closely as possible the Interaction and patterns of influence between the traditional and the modernized segments of the society.

Among others, the followlng two clusters of structural variables appear significant :

1. *The basic patterns of social relationship*, with special reference to affectivity vs. affective neutrality; self-orientation vs. collectivity—orientation; universalism vs. particularism; achievement vs. ascription; and specificity diffuseness.

2. *The nature of social structure*, with special reference to close-knit or loose structuring of the system; types of groups, associations, and other units of social structure; gap between the elite and the masses; patterns of interaction between the folk, the peasant, and the urban elements of society; "reference groups" in society; and the operation of socialisation, surveillance and consensus mechanisms in society.

Most developing societies have achieved political sovereignty after bitterly-fought anti-colonial struggles. In consequence, their policies—both pre-independence and post-independance – have tended to have strong ideological overtones; and even today their ideological emphases are significant. Ideology can be a strong stimulant to change, but it can also lead to excesses that can, in the long run, prove detrimental to the objectives of development and progress. Formal statements of ideology are often misleading for, their expressions in internal, national, and local contexts are often remarkably different. The ideology of the revolutionary elite is quite often different from that of other elites, and the gap between the ideology of the elites and that of the masses is indeed wide. Because of poor articulation many contradictions and paradoxes operate behind the facade of unity in their ideology. Their influence on the programmes of change merits serious note.

It can be stated axiomatically that a modern society is characterised by empathy, mobility, and high participation. The individual, in these societies, possesses strong secular aspirations; his achievement motivation is relatively uninhibited by ritual considerations. In other words, he is able to compute strategies on a broad stage. The highly participant character of such a society permits the individual for wide situational and motivational choice. Thus, the transition from tradition to modernity involves a fundamental change of values.

Planning for change, cannot, therefore, omit a consideration of the traditional and the transitional values of a developing society.

The following value constellations in this context, are important : cultural orientation to nature, supernature, time, space, and man; values concerning work, leisure and wealth; and values relating to change, especially those regarding different kinds of change. The differentials in the different developing societies are likely to affect significantly the content, the tone, and the pace of their plans for development.

The Economic Context

Most plans of national development set for themselves carefully worked out economic objectives. Community development, although aims at well-rounded and manysided development of communities, cannot ignore the economic compulsions; in fact, its success is often judged by its economic results. As is well known, economic development and social change stimulate each other, and we can, therefore, assume, that without acceleration of economic progress, plans for cultural development will not succeed beyond a point. The economic context of planned change thus acquires a special significance.

Poverty characterises all developing societies. Their per capita income is invariably low. In consequence, the level of savings for productive investment cannot be high. Most of these societies are mainly agricultural. From the technological angle, agriculture and its allied industries have progressed little from a primitive level. Their economies have a disproportionately large subsistence sector; in fact, the primary production sector dominates the economy. The progress of agriculture is greatly hampered; while the total land area available for agriculture cannot be appreciably increased, the pressure of population mainly dependent on agriculture is increasing every year. The requirements of the increased population that depends directly or indirectly on agriculture outweigh the small benefits in terms of additional production gained through the introduction of limited technological innvovations in this field.

This is however, only a general picture of the prevailing economic situation. Transition is in evidence in this sphere also. Many developing societies have signficant pockets of modern economy, but their size is not large. In general, the traditional and the modern sectors are not well integrated. The industrial sector, in most of these countries, continues to be dominated by the trader-producer who has so far failed to develop an industrial ethic.

Here also one finds pronounced difference in the economic base, the economic ideology, and the economic values of the different countries, and some glaring contrasts exist within individual countries themselves.

The differentials are accounted for as follows :

In the economic base by the ownership and distribution of of the means of production (especially agriculture), the distribution of economic power, the technological levels of agriculture and other industries, and the degree of integration between traditional and modern sectors of economy; in the economic ideology by orientation to communism, democratic socialism, or capitalism; the degree of articulation of the predominant ideology accepted by the government; factors balancing and holding in check the contending doctrines; and attitudes towards planning; in the ceonomic values—by the material valuations of the people (generally and also by strata); the attitudes towards work, wealth, savings, and risk-taking; the levels of aspiration and avenues of achievement; and the economic discipline and sense of responsibility.

The economic texture of developing societies is a complex weave of these elements. The combination of different elements in each case imparts to it an individuality. Programmes of national development, and of community development, therefore, have to be devised to suit each specific case.

The Political Context

In operational terms, the political context of development is perhaps the most important because in the developing societies almost all the major decisions concerning development are political decisions. Politics is emerging as the dominant theme of the new nations. In some of these countries, political decisions have been tended to over-ride the hard economic and social realities of the situation. Such adventures have often not produced the desired economic development, but there is still no evidence of any repentence on the part of those who seek to order change by flamboyant political fiats. Even where conditions are not so extreme, the planning apparatus can rarely claim autonomy; its policies have to be guided invariably by political exigencies and compulsions. The political situation thus sets the tune of national development. This necessitates a clear understanding of the political cultures and political idioms of the developing area.

Not all the countries which set out as free nations to become 'democratic states' have been able to keep themselves steadily on the path of democracy. Some have succumbed to one party—and in many ways one person—rule; some others now have disguised or undisguised military dictatorships. Lack of political maturity and impatience with the teething troubles of democracy were perhaps at the back of their deviation from the chosen path. In some countries there is evidence of a return to democracy—at this state, in a limited form—from dictatorship or from Communism (such as Romania, East Germany, Chekoslovakia, Poland). Even those who have some remained faithful to democracy—both in form and spirit—have had some disconcerting experiences.

In varying degrees, the political cultures of developing societies share some of the following characteristics :

One, in tone and temper their politics is geared more to agitation and revolt than to nation-building. The leaders who performed their solidarity-building roles very creditably, are finding it some what difficult to adapt themselves to their new problem-solving roles.

Two, politics in these countries around individuals. This explains the prevalence of cliques, factions, resource groups, and resource networks as key elements of the political network.

Three, political roles tend to merge with social and personal roles. This will perhaps explain why the patron and broker functions of leadership in these countries are so important.

Four, political opinion in regard to specific issues lacks cohesion. A major contradiction is presented by the gap between revolutionary world-views on international questions and very narrow and parochial views on domestic matters.

Five, the political process itself lacks organic unity. This is accounted for by a low degree of interest articulation and interest aggregation, and ineffective political communication.

Six, their cultural, economic, and political goals are often not in sharp focus. A considerable degree of confusion can be attributed to the presence of a two way ambivalence to both tradition and modernity.

And, lastly, while the rights of freedom are well recognised, constraints and responsibilities are not. In consequence, political discipline is poorly developed.

These characteristics notwithstanding, there are significant differences in the ethos and the idiom of politics in the developing societies. The political emphases of particular systems have to be understood clearly because of their dominant influence on the objectives of planning and strategies of plan implementation.

The Administrative Context

To the administrative machine of the developing countries, large scale handling of developmental operations is a comparatively new experience. By tradition and training it was geared more to the efficient collection of revenue and maintenance of law and order than to the administration of gigantic programmes of welfare. The tasks of development have necessitated certain basic adjustments in its outlook and approach; the dislocation of established bureaucratic norms is imminent, and new norms to replace them are yet to emerge. In many ways, the first decade of development has been a period of great trial for the bureaucracy; it has not only had to grapple with problems in an area in which it lacked experience, it has also to work under unforeseen pressures ofpolitics and public opinion. In the process, in most countries it lost some of the power, prestige, and privileges that it enjoyed in the colonial past. Its aloofness from the masses was considerably broken down; it could no longer afford to have a paternal and patronizing attitude to them. In the context of development, administrative procedures and techniques also had to undergo major modifications. The bureaucracy's response to these challenges in many countries was commendable, but its reservations and resistence, and its doubts and cynicism have proposed some important problems for the formulation and implementation of development programmes.

The indispensability of the bureaucracy is recognised, but at the same time it is felt that a change in its ways of thought and work is also essential. Limited attempts have been made to effect these changes through programmes of orientation and training and through reorganisation of the administrative pattern. To enable the administrative machine to function effectively and efficiently for the speedy implementation of development programmes, some conutries are attempting thorough going administrative reforms. The orientation and training programmes as well as the administrative reforms have some clear objectives :

> They are principally aimed at loosening the rigidity of the administrative structure, democratising the decision-making processes, and quickening the pace of administrative action. It is undeniable that the administrative context is a powerful determinant of the content and direction of community development programmes.

The major contexts of community development, therefore, have been discussed here only to emphasise that successful experiments in one set of conditions cannot always be duplicated in another set of conditions. The emphasis is not misplaced because there is a noticeable tendency among developing countries to do so. The approach is the essence of community development; external forms may vary according to the demands of specific situations—the people, the resources etc.

Lastly, to stimulate the process of planned change certain investments are necessary. The more important among them are the investments in building the social and economic infrastructures of development; fostering an image of the future which promises the attainment of increasingly higher standards of living; developing attitudes conducive to sustained economic growth and social progress; creating resources and skills required for continuous development; and promoting institutions that can effectively assume responsibility for carrying forward the development programme.

2. Sociological Perspective of Technology Generation in Agriculture

If one contemplates to construct a theory of technology generation in agriculture, he must consider a wide variety of factors with varying relative emphases, such as :

1. relative factor endowments and scarcities (e.g., land, labour, capital and water);
2. export orientation versus domestic consumption;
3. vested interests of farming populations and their political clout. and organized lobbying;
4. market distortions and factor and product prices;
5. fads, biases and predilections of policy makers and research managers;
6. existing stage of technology and scientific manpower;
7. science-related overheads and infrastructure; and
8. professional and personal orientations, commitments and interests of agricultural scientists.

Thus, one can come up with a largely economic theory of technology generation, or a purely managerial and human relations theory, or a political economy theory, or a social and psychological theory, depending upon the relative importance accorded to the various factors.

A sociology of knowledge framework, which treats technological change as a special variant of social change, seeks to offer a comprehensive, synthetic, holistic perspective attempting to integrate the various sets of determinants of technological change. In this framework the agricultural scientist, the science and technology he creates, and his professional behaviour, values and interests are all socially situated. In a framework of this kind, it is not safe or valid to assume that agricultural technologies generated are entirely or strictly in conformity with the perceptions and estimations of user needs, capacities, conditions and priorities.

Particularly in a Third World country like India, characterised by skewed land distribution, preponderance of small and marginal operators, adverse man-land ratios, and subsistence farming systems, technology generation process would rarely be free of latent and manifest distortions. This situation obtains for the simple reason that marginalised subsistence sectors of Indian agriculture, scattered all over, and indigent and unorganized, have not yet constituted powerful pressure groups to architects of technology policies, technology makers and research administrators. There is as yet no impressive evidence of direct participation of this section of agricultural community in the technology creation or generation processes. Their needs, problems and interests are if at all, indirectly communicated by their so-called spokesmen—the field extension personnel, and to a large extent by the members of the fourth estate, journalists and agricultural correspondents. For all practical purposes, no viable, assertive and articulate cooperative movement is emerging, and the political parties that espouse their interests are weaklings on the political scene. The glaring case of the dryland agricultural sector in India substantiates this contention. Although this sector is predominant in terms of area and population, it received till now only five to seven per cent of the total research budgets of the Indian Council of Agricultural Research (ICAR). It is only in the last few years or so this sector is being accorded the attention it deserves in research and policy making circles and even so a reasonable surmise is that the dry sector is attracting notice for no other reason than the shortfall in pulses and oilseeds production and the consequent high prices and import bills.

Attributes of Agriculture

In contrast to other productive enterprises, agriculture presents a few outstanding attributes. The most prominent of them is the agro-climatic heterogeneity. Agriculture is a techno-economic activity characterised by immense diversity of farming situations all over the world. The diversity owes mainly to three factors : its anciency; its dependency on nature; and its global diffusion. Dependent on nature, agriculture's diversity parallels nature's diversity. As the art and craft to produce food, fuel, fodder and fibre, agriculture is caught up in a eomplex eco-system-water-soil-plant-seed-climate-insects and micro-organisms of nature.

Agricultural technology concerns the use and management of this factor matrix and their interactive relationships (Zimmerman, 1971). Further, Zimmerman (1971) writes, a griculture concedes to nature the dominant role in man's productive efforts. In it man has not gained the upper hand; nature remains the master and man is only the helper. Man's managerial ability and control decreases progressively from, say, water and soil to insects and micro-organisms and the biotic energies of plants and animals, to climate (temperature, rain, wind and solar radiation). Modern agriculture may increasingly come under the spell of machines, science, industry and commerce, but it cannot be wholly absorbed by them as many ecologists and agricultural scientists say. Agriculture retains an irreducible residual dependence on living nature. This is best illustrated by plant and animal responses at various levels—cellular and intracellular, biochemical, physiological and yield levels—to pollutants and agro-chemicals.

A second critical attribute of agriculture is that cultural and socio-economic heterogeneity overlays its natural diversity. The direct consequence of anciency and the global diffusion of agriculture is that it is practised not only under every conceivable combination of natural factors but also under a vast diversity of socio-economic conditions and cultural institutions. The cultural and socio-economic heterogeneity interlocks with the eco-system diversity in agriculture. Technological possibilities and outcomes are constrained by this overlay of heterogeneities of farming system.

The third outstanding attribute of agriculture is the highly privatized character of the production decisions, skills and behaviours of millions of farm producers. Naturally, technology generation, technology acceptance and technology diffusion are affected and complicated by these attributes or features of agriculture, whereas the natural diversities preclude possibilities of generation of universal agricultural technologies and impose the harsh condition that a workable technology must necessarily be crop—and locality—specific. The agronomic and socio-economic heterogeneity, and individual farm decision-making restrict the diffusion and adoption of specific kinds of technology packages.

Again, agro-climatic and socio-economic heterogeneity and privatized decisions together produce a situation in which it may be safely hypothesized that where field extension agency net works are more effectively established and organized in servicing the needs of technology producers and technology users, there is a greater chance for diverse and appropriate technologies to be forged from the laboratories because of more efficient land-to-lab feed back. The three attributes of agriculture discussed above suggest the need for building up a strong organizational base of triadic relations among farmers, agricultural scientists and extension personnel.

Land to Lab Feedback

Agricultural research tends to become more dynamic, diverse and innovative because of grass roots planning. It helps overcome homophily in communicative behaviour and enables the scientist to assess and define the user needs more accurately and continuously in terms of required research operations, reorientations, and adaptations.

Furthermore, the altenative system helps the scientist aecquire a holistic picture of the problem situation. Modernization of agriculture, thus, depends as heavily upon effectively meeting the field informational needs of farm scientists as it depends upon lab-to-land information transfer. This is the crux of the communication problem of technological development in agriculture (Lionberger and Chang, 1970).

An efficient farm information system therefore, is one that constantly endeavours to sustain and upgrade the credibility of agricultural research by continuous and direct exposure of agricultural scientists to farm-orien-originated stimuli, ideas, challenges and possibilities.

The common experience of those dealing with agricultural development is that agricultural scientists have a tendency to take the farmer for granted. The assumptions underlying their research planning and priorities may be uninformed or even mis-informed. Scientists are reluctant to work at the hardest end of the research spectrum where quick results are not possible. They have a tendency to develop vested interest in a specific research scheme affecting their security, survival and career prospects. There was no broad-based development of agricultural research to give technology support proportionately to all areas and all important crops.

Multiple Research Goals

Attempts have been made, especially by economists, to measure returns to investment in agricultural research, cropwise and country-wise for specified periods, since it is generally believed that agricultural research represented a relatively better investment opportunity than other developmental investments (Arndt and Ruttan, 1975). While several of the estimates of returns to agricultural research are questionable on grounds, of accuracy, methodology, and subjectivity, it is argued that, as quantitative measures they are neuertheless useful to monitor performance of agricultural research.

From the returns point of view, three ways by which agricultural research contributes are (a) in finding out ways and means of reducing production costs (b) in determining the combination of practices and inputs that increase yields; (c) in developing the most efficient post-harvest technologies for processing and storage, preservation, and marketing of products to enable the farmers to reap the benefits of higher prices. Agricultural research may also be directed towards increasing labour employment, monitoring, changes in natural systems—consequence of farming, changes in soils, nutrient cycles, flora and fauna and agro-ecosystems. Yet another fruitful avenue of research is the exploration of land use systems and their impact on health, ecology and socio-economic conditions of the local populations. The focus on economic returns to research costs appears a narrow concern viewed in the light of this broad spectrum of objectives of agricultural research. Making a critical note of India's agricultural experience, noted economist, Hanumantha Rao (1986) observes that the present yield-increasing, land-saving agricultural technology is and, also labour-saving hence, not suitable for large tracts of the country characterized by low investment and risk-bearing capacity. What is needed is a technology which raises the total output per unit of land from all crops through multiple cropping augmenting intensity and labour absorbtion. The scientific infrastructure borrowed by the developing economies is conditioned by the factor-use biases of the developed economies.

Two major issues of modern agricultural technology, in general, draw special attention. These concern (a) yield gaps and yield variations and (b) stability of adoption behaviour of farmers. Experience with improved dryland agricultural technology shows considerable slippages in yields from research farms to farmer's fields, from verification trials on farmer's fields to demonstration farms, from demonstration farms to progressive farmers' fields, and between ordinary farms. Such yield gaps, induced by climate, cultural and managerial practices, soil conditions, farm size, and technology, are observed between different plots of the same farmer, and between different farms within the same agro-climatic zone. Much of this could be attributed to technology recommended. Graded and variable technologies rather than uniform technology packages are an answer to this problem. The development of graded and variable technologies requires direct exposure of agricultural scientists to farmer's situations.

The second issue of modern agricultural technology refers to role-switching behaviour of farmers who may be classified as adopters, partial adopters, non-adopters, and so on. A total adopter is one who adopts the entire package at recommended levels. He may not commit all his land to the new technology. He is like the adopter at the trial stage of adoption. On the contrary, a partial adopter accepts only a few of the recommended practices or uses them at adjusted or modified levels. He may again, be a full-scale or limited-scale partial adopter. A total or partial adopter may, in course of time turn into non-adopter by discontinuation of the technology. Thus, adopters, partial-adopters and non-adopters, are not fixed categories or have stable roles. This role-switching behaviour of farmers provides a crucial test of the success and failure of technology. Success involves conversion from partial and non-adoption to total full-scale adoption of the largest number of potential adopters. A conversion experience in the reverse order is disastrous to extension work. The change-over from adoption to non-adoption calls into question the validity, viability, stability and profitability of the recommended technonology. It also undermines the credibility of agricultural research and extension. Therefore, the trialability and compatibility of a new technology and its associated post-harvest problems including prices, should be carefully assessed by teams of farm scientists, economists, and sociologists. A diachronic, multi-faceted framework of investigation of agricultural technologies will be called for. No technological breakthrough in agriculture can become revolutionary unless role-switching takes place in the desired direction on a large scale and sustained basis.

Implications of New Technology

The kind of technology developed and put through the delivery system currently for use by farmers is a bio-chemical, seed-fertilizer-pesticide package. This technological package is just one coordinate of the total production system. The other coordinates are the farmer; the hierarchical socio-economic structure of the agrarian society; the ecological and the geo-climatic factor; product markets; the public policy (Subsiders, price supports, levy, public procurement and distribution, internal movement of produce and external exports, etc.); and lastly the social over-heads (extansion service, storage, power, roads, transport, and marketing). The adoption of this technology meant two dislocated events for farmers; replacement of traditional farming practices and incorporation of primary producers into a wider network of relations and dependency. In the earlier farming system, the farm input requirements were met by the farmer from within his own farm and village resources. This feature was dissolved and the farmer is drawn out of the circle of his traditional relationships and institutions into a new and more complicated nexus of relationships and institutional arrangements. The traditional farmer could raise the needed seed on his own farm or procure it from neighbours. In case of new technology adoption, the dependency on outside agencies created a situation of uncertainty with untimely or inadequate supply or poor quality of seed affecting cropping schedule and performance. It made him vulnerable to exploitation.

There are also other problems associated with the high yielding varieties of agricultural crops. These improved varieties have a higher vulnerability to insects and diseases. They are more sensitive and cannot withstand stress conditions (soil salinity alkalinity, and lack of soil moisture, etc.). They cannot be adopted independently but must be accompanied by complimentary and agronomic practices. Thus, they multiply costs and inputs. They alter the ecology of the farming systems. High yielding varieties bred for tolerance of a wider variation in geo-climatic conditions tend to alter crop profiles and species diversity very essential to healthy ecological feedback mechanisms and delicate unknown ecological balances. Farming in monocultural situation causes many local species and varieties to become extinct, thereby narrowing the range and diversity of natural genetic variation necessary for breeding purposes. Hybridisation thus poses newer and unpredictable challenges. It necessitates effective pest and disease surveilllance plans. Lack of specificity in varietal improvement is another problem. This accounts for the high rate of drop-out and rejection of a large number of released crop varieties.

Lack of specificity of HYVs is perhaps the reason for their vulnerability to pests and diseases and their genetic instability and fluctuations in yields. Established traditional varieties, selected and adapted through the operation of the Natural Selection Process over long periods of time in particular agro-climatic situations, were characterised by high local-ecological specificity and had superior genetic ability, pest and disease resistance, and capacity to withstand other locality—specific stress factors (e.g. drought, water-logging, soil acidity and micro-nutrient deficiencies, etc). And therefore, throughout the world the greatest need for indigenous technical knowledge for sustainable agriculture has been felt.

3. Extension Approach in Rural Development

The extension approach in rural development was first introduced in community development, containing welfare aims and socio-economic change through self-help and self-reliance techniques. The basic idea which influences the thinking of planners was the so called "multi-purpose approach" of extension based on the principle of all round development. In order to implement the multi-purpose programme of action, the most significant contribution of the Community Development Programme was the Extension Organizations' set up with the provision of multi-purpose village level workers to function at the grassroot level as a link between block extension administration and the rural people. But such all round develop ment effort can only be successful when :

1. there is no resource constraints,
2. all needs are equally urgent and
3. there is some kind of logic in the rural environment which makes attainment of single and impossible without the simultaneous attainment of all others.

None of the above premises, however hold good in the present context of extension strategy for agricultural development.

Under the serious resource constraints multi-purpose approach with its multi-sectoral constraints directed at a wide spectrum of rural population could not make much headway. Agrlculture, the most important sector of the national economy, was neglected and food production suffered. This has lead to the diversification of more "limited purpose" approach with its concentration on the more dominant aspects of economic development, i.e., the increase in agricultural production. Thus, the multipurpose approach yielded place to a limited-purpose approach, what may be called the "target sector approach." In this approach, Community Development objective came to be subordinated to the objective of increasing agricultural production. From this period onwards, there started an element of direct technological intervention in the extension set up of the country.

The assumptions made in all the multipurpose and target sector approaches that the available technology applicable to best areas are adequate for bringing about development of rural people in general was not tenable. So technology relevant to specific defficient areas as well as target groups have to be generated. Mere reorganization of the extension efforts is not and will not be the answer.

Further, the extension programme must have limited attainable goals with professionally trained and competent extension personnel. The extension personnel should have clear cut area of jurisdication with a number of families whom they can conveniently reach. And also they should have support of materials and other important inputs needed for adoptation of an innovation by the farmers. The use of various inputs like fertilizers, plant protection methods and modernisation, etc., cannot stand in isolation. Besides, the farmers' cognitive orientation towards input was conditioned by firstly from the profitability of the available technology accompanying the inputs. And secondly, the physical and economic access of the farmers to such inputs.

Considering all above, it may be said that the extension programme's one of the major weaknesses is very thin in formation-base, particularly at the farmers level of various strata within a region as well as inter-regional levels on which to develop an extension programme. The basic questions of why a farmer adopts a particular innovation or technology is still largely a mistery. Definitely, economics provides a glaring answer. The cultivator will adopt clearly a profitable innovation. However, there is obviously the more than this and to achieve rural development objectives the extension programme must be smoothen and appropriate to fit into the socio-cultural and agro-economic systems in which a farmer lives and extension agent tries to change the farmer's behaviour.

A New Approach to Community Development

The need of the day is an objective examination of the actual realities in rural areas and to make plans on the basis of such a study. The primary aim of such examination should be to develop scientific concepts of a community and of a region. So far, the extension administrative units, the district, sub-division, taluk, thana, block and the village have been used as unit for development. For administrative purposes, these arbitrary units may be useful but for integrated and balanced development we need a new set of boundaries based on a scientific delineation of the community and the recipient at the micro level. It is one of the axioms of the economics of location, human geography and rural sociology that lot of services can be obtained in all settlements. A small population can support only the minimum services needed for day-to-day living. On the other hand a large population can support too many specialised services. With economic development and input transport more demands are generated for specialised services. Thus, a new concept of community is posited in which a higher order centre becomes a nucleus of a hinterland consisting of several villages. A whole hierarchy is obtained when one observes the emergence of settlement which offer progressively more specialised services. On a continuum of service specialisation, with the small village and the large metropolitan city representing two opposite poles, a whole range of settlement can be arrayed. Each settlement has its own area of influence or hinterland the size of which increases with the degree of specialization in the central settlement. Such settlements which are nuclei or central to their hinterlands have been defined as "growth centres" by location theorists. The hinterlands of such growth centres do not necessarily coincide with the existing administrative boundaries. The use of the existing administrative boundaries the geographic framework for reasources allocation may, therefore, lead more imbalances rather than reducing it and also extension services become difficult and unrealistic.

Rural Growth Centre for Larger Benefit to People

The growth centre concept for the whole village development is not new in India, although in the past, not enough attention was given to it. It has been revived only during 70s as an important strategy of rural development. The economic relationships between the town and the surrounding villages was suggested to be one of mutual dependence. The villages would produce raw materials and food for the town. In return, the town will process these materials and send them back to the villages in finished form Machineries and their servicing would also to be provided by the town. But present Planning Commission does not consider at all this concept for planning purposes.

The available theories and methods for identifying growth centres for all round rural development of various orders and their hinterlands could be utilised for the planning and development of rural areas. One that may suit our purposes very well is the 'Central Place Theory.' There are alternative theories also which need to be tested under Indian conditions. The concept of central place theory is mainly a contribution of a German Geographer Christaller (1933) and has been refined and improved upon by Losch and others (1945). The theory is deductive but was tested by countries in Southern Germany and by others in different parts of the world. The gist of Christaller's theory stripped of details and elaboration is as follows :

1. A Central Place (usually a city or a town depending on the specific area or region in city) which provides functions and services to its tributory area, is located at the centre of minimum aggregate travel providing minimum cost to the customers and maximum profit to the sellers.

2. There is a hierarchy of such central places. The higher order places private function which lower order places do not have. But the reverse is not true. Higher order place provide functions in addition to what the lower order places have.

3. Functions which are unique to higher order places have a wide range (geographical area of influence) than those which are common to both higher and lower order places.

4. The higher order places are fewer and more widely spaced than lower order places.

5. Higher order places not only have their unique functions, but have a larger number of institutions providing lower order functions than do the lower order places.

6. There is a step by step hierarchy of central places ranging from the higher order place to the lowest order place with each order of place "nesting" the next lower order places.

According to Christaller, centrality of a place is a measure of its importance. He recognises population size as an associative factor but the major emphasis is placed on the functional importance of a place in terms of the nature and the range of services offered.

The concept of growth centres, therefore, provides a methodology for a balanced programme of rural development. If the central place theory has formulated by Christaller revived by others is realised, the field investigation will indicate a hierarchy of settlements and their hinterlands based on the progressive specialization of functions in each settlement.

First, the lack of enough resources and the need for consolidation of resources in selected places.

Second, the lack of scientific guidelines for selecting places which are ideally located for regenerating the entire countryside.

There is also need for decentralising economic activities so that the benefits of economic development can be shared by all groups and all regions. And the scientifically selected growth centres at various levels would provide such locations. Emperical research could easily provide quidelines for :

1. The location of different order of services and of investment on specific projects;
2. Delineation of viable communities, sub-regions, and regions; and
3. Planning for future growth centres which will be needed in a rapidly changing agricultural scene.

Hence, extension approach for agricultural and rural development will be easier and meaningfully purposeful to reach and cover almost all the people of all the regions effectively.

References

Arundt, T.M. and V.W. Ruttan, 1975. Resource Allocation and Productivity in National and International Agricultural Research—A Seminar Report, Research and Trainging Network Publications, N.Y., The Agricultural Development Council, inc.

Christaller, W. 1933. *The Central Places of Southern Germany* (Translated by C. Baskin), Eaglewood Chiffs, N.J., (1966).

Hanumanth Rao, C.H. 1986. Science and Technology Policy : An Overall View and Broader Implications, *Indian Journal of Agricuvtural Economics*, 41 (3).

Lionberger, H.F. and H.C. Chang, 1970. *Farm Information for Modernising Agriculture : The Taiwan System*, Preager Special Studies in International Economics and Development, N.Y., Praeger Publishers.

Losch, A. 1954. Economics of Location (Ttranslated by W.H. Waglom and W.F. Stolper), New Haven.

Zimmerman, E.W. 1971. The Nature of Agriculture in Raymond E. Borton (ed): *Selected Readings, to accompany Getting Agriculture Moving*, Vol. 1, N.Y. The Agriculture Development Council, Inc.

FIVE

Role of Extension and Training for Agricultural and Rural Development

With the changing scenario of global agriculture, today improved agricultural technology and practices are availble for use by many farmers in most developing countries. For resource poor farmers, particularly in Africa and Asia, improved technologies need not involve at the beginning any additional purchased inputs, but rather better husbandry practices. For more sophisticated farmers more complex technologies can be advised and introduced.

One of the constraints to introduce such technology is the lack of mechanisms to learn what are the main constraints and needs of the farmers and to transmit new and pratical relevant knowledge to them. This is beeause most existing extension systems in developing countries have been poorly managed and disorganised, and depend on poorly trained and motivated extension workers. Knowledge has not therefore, been effectively transmitted both ways : from farmers to research and vice-versa. When such knowledge begins to be effectively transmitted and to stimulate productivity improvements, demands by farmers for more knowledge, for farm inputs, for credit and other services increases. It follows that if extension can be made to work, a significant impact on agriculture can be obtained.

The basic solution of the agricultural extension problem is to improve the organisation and the management of national extension services with the participation of and in close coperation with the farmers themselves.

Considering the present changing perspective of farmers' aspirations and agricultural scenario throughout the world the basic needs of agricultural extension and training should follow some fundamental principles in relation to extension or agricultural innovation and training needs of farmers, such as :

(i) Extension service should aim to be able to provide advice on all farmers' agricultural enterprises such as field crops, tree crops, livestock and inland fisheries.

(ii) There must be continuous agricultural training for all staff in the extension service in order to increase their professionalism. Training must be practical. Demonstrations in the field should be used as a major training tool.

(iii) A premium is put on gathering from farmers existing knowhow and developing new extension messages.

(iv) Farmers needs are ascertained and agricultural knowledge is communicated by extension agents to the maximum number of farmers possible.

(v) The management system which relies on a fixed routing for farmers, extension staff and their supervisors ensures that extension agents actually visit farmers.

(vi) The extension system need to be national in scope. The goal should be to consolidate these various systems into national extension programmes which are streamlined, efficient, and cheaper than the agregate of the independent confused systems. A concentrated effort is required to make an extension structure work in a country as a whole.

(vii) In Africa and some of the countries of Asia, it is becoming increasingly clear that efforts must focus on improving local capacity to manage extension, rather than relying on foreign management. Foreign management is not sustainable, foreigners eventually leave, and the development process suffers.

(viii) In designing an extension system, contact with farmers, their active participation and the determination of farmers' need for technology are critical. The design must emphasize the role of field staff contact with farmers and the critical need to obtain feedback from the latter so that extension and research can respond to their real needs.

(ix) Support to extension system should be designed with a long term perspective (10 to 15 years atleast), not limited to the traditional five-year project cycle.

(x) A political commitment is of fundamental importance for the success of the extension programme in any country. Without such commitment, sustainable results are unlikely.

Agricultural research systems also need considerable strengthening if not total rehabilitation in some countries. More efficient extension is therefore only part, of course an important part, of the solution.

The African and Asian countries, though, are on quite different levels of economic, social and organizational development, they share a number of common characteristics. Compare to the industrialised countries, these are low per capita income of the population, low labour productivity, preponderence of the primary sector in the economy, shortage of capital for investment, disparities in income and inaccess to economic and educational resources, low educational level of the masses of people, especially in the rural population, and high rate of population growth. All the countries have however, a considerable development potential.

Extension, therefore has to face a variety of situational factors which influence concepts and programmes. There is, first, the political situation in the country. The majority of the countries of both African and Asian continents belong to the type of market economies with a liberal political and economic system. They aim in general at developing individual, small and medium size farm holdings, using a number of development instruments designed for voluntary participation of the farming population and they try to bring out structural changes through more or less cautious reforms.

Again, the rural development concepts differ to some degree from country to country. The self-help and peoples' participation component plays a more or less important role. In the majority of countries of both Africa and Asia, "Sectoral approach" to rural development based on concentration on a few important agricultural activities is followed. Some countries have persued an "integrated approach" to rural development which is more complex and tries to coordinate largely on regional basis, efforts in agriculture, rural industrialisation, improvement of infrastructure, health and education. The functioning and organization of extension and training differ in the two types.

The technological level reached already in rural areas influences the systems quite strongly. Land and labour productivity depend to a large degree of capital input, agricultural research output and on the skills of the agricultural workers. Moreover, availability of communication systems and infrastructure development are important factors.

It is also evident that the rural structure has a high impact on organisation and programmes of extension and training systems. The density of population and settlements differs quite strongly. It is, in general, higher in Asia than in African countries. Apparently, higher density facilitates extension work in many respects, and this all the more so as the road and transport systems are better developed in such cases. The approach to extension depends also largely on characteristics of land tenure and agrarian structure. Further, farm size availability of energy, water, and other inputs determine the content of extension work quite strangly. Where farm families have less than one hectare of un-irrigated land and manual labour is the exclusive energy source extension agents must bear in mind, when making recommendations, the fact that farmers may have real or no marketable surplus.

Reviewing critically the above changing world agricultural senario and needs of agricultural extension and training for the farmers of 2000 AD, this chapter intends to discuss the different perspectives of agricultural extension and training for extension personnel and farmers to meet the agricultural development challenges in the coming decade and beyond on three different heads :

1. Features of Agricultural Extension and Training;
2. Organisational Support for Effective Agricultural Extension and Training; and
3. Constraints in Agricultural Extension and Training.

1. Features of Agricultural Extension and Training

Training of Extension Personnel is an integral part of agricultural production programme and embraces the entire extension agency from the village level to the state level with a view to build up their professional competencies.

The existing level of general education, farming knowledge and skills in the farming population must be taken into consideration by extension and training agencies too. Where the majority of the adult farmers are literate, which is the case in a number of countries in Asia and the North East and where average farming practices are scientifically based already, agricultural training requires highly qualified staff, and an on-going transmission of new research findings to the farmers. However as the level of knowledge and the interest in modern farming regularly differ strongly within the farming community, problem becomes acute as to how to deal with different target groups.

The economic policy framework, therefore, plays an important part in successful extension work. This work will be the more facilitated, the more productive and input prices and marketing conditions are favourable for farmers in those spheres of which extension activities concentrate. The Government have not always realised that extension activities cannot substitute a positive price policy. No extension service will bring about a broad and lasting adpotion of new crops or other innovative practices, unless these are economically more remunerative to the farmers than the practices applied hitherto. The varying degree of coordination between price and marketing policy on the one hand and support services policy on the other explain to some extent, the difference in extension efficiency prevail from country to country.

Role of Extension and Training in Agriculture and Rural Development

The importance of extension and training for agricultural and rural development has been valued quite differently in the course of time and in different countries. The more technical change has been recognised as a major prerequisite of development, the better it has been realised that process of research results and dissemination of the new knowledge of farmers cannot adequately take place through direct contacts between researchers and farmers : there is a greater awareness that the task is being solved better by an advisory service which develops an extension strategy and use a specific set of methods for fast communication of recommendations and for inducing farmers to action. It has also been realised in all countries that the human factor is most essential in the development process. Extension and training agencies which have largely educational functions have come to receive greater recognition than they had in the past as regards the independent nature of the activities.

Whatever development strategy is applied there is rather unanimous agreement today that agricultural extension and training have an important role to play in the improvement of farming in developing countries. Extension services render possible direct contact with the most of the farmers. Sometimes, especially in remote areas, they are the only direct contact between the government's development agencies and the villagers. Extension is, in principle, a flexible instrument which can be adapted to varying conditions. As educational instruments, extension and training operate in a sphere relatively underdeveloped in villages.

In different political and socio-economic systems, the functions and roles of extension and training staff may be defined quite differently. In countries with a centrally controlled economy and extension services will be taken as a mere instrnment of government policy : the extension agents' primary tasks are to enforce the attainment of quantitative targets set by the government and to help in educating farmers. The supervisory component is some times stronger than the educational one. The opposite pattern is found in the western industrialised countries. Here, the principle has long been recognised that the extension agent's main task is to assist the farmers and look after their interests but not to impose government plans as a matter of policy.

Agricultural Extension Objectives

Way back in 1959, some pioneer workers in the field of extension, while working in Sudan for rural development, have made a comprehensive list of objectives of extension (Von Blanckenburg, 1984), These are—

(i) Promotion of out-of-school education for the rural people to help them to improve their total situation by enabling them to get in close touch with agricultural knowledge.

(ii) Helping the rural people to recognise their needs and wants and to enable them to play active roles in solving those problems and meeting those needs.

(iii) Influencing the rural people and motivating them to find better means and ways to promote their conditions and attain higher levels of living.

(iv) Helping the rural people to gain new skills and adopt new and better attitudes towards various aspects of living.

(v) Helping the rural women to gain new knowledge and skills related to home making, home economics, and child care.

(iv) Helping educate the rural youth to become self-reliant in solving their problems and meeting the challenges of their environment.

In 1974, the following additional objectives for extension work in the Sudan where further listed :

I. Raising the level of productivity of the farmer and familiarizing him with the various options available to him.

II. Freeing the farmer from traditionalism by teaching him new concepts and better habits.

III. Establishing training facilities for the use of the farmer.

IV. Preparing leader cadres of technicians to shoulder the responsibilities listed in I, II and III above.

V. Focusing the state's attention on the most pressing problems of the rural people to ensure greater financial support for extension work.

VI. Publicizing and generalizing the successes achieved at certain places to less fortunate areas in other parts of the country to multiply their positive efforts.

VII. Exerting the greatest effort to place the results of research in the hands of the farmer so that no gap in his level of knowledge and performance would develop as to hamper the application of science to his farming operations (Von Blackenburg, 1984).

These two lists of objectives though were meant considering the infrastructure, resources and aspirations of Sudanees farmers these broad based objectives are applicable to other developing countries both in Africa and Asia. The first list concentrates on the non-formal education aspects : information, teaching skills and changing attitudes. The second stresses the task of extension to raise agricultural productivity and to bring about application of science and research findings to farming. Moreover, training of farmers and extension staff is emphasized.

2. Organisational Support for Agricultural Extension and Training

For the successful implementation of the Farmers Training and Education Programme minimum necessary organisational support should be provided ut the State as well as at National level. This support will be in terms of providing equipment, production of audio visuals, like; film strips, provision of publicity van and other educational aids. Similarly, at the national level, there will be staff for providing essential guidance, organising training programme for trainers at the state and field levels and training in effective communication methods and media, securing coordination between different agencies. In order to provide effective coordination at the district level in the implementation of farmers' training programme, the appointment of a District Training Officer in each of the Farmers Training districts, is must.

Thus, the proposed Farmers' Training and Education Programme through audio-visual aids outlined above will meet the growing needs of the farmers and other changing agricultural scenario of the nation. The demonstrations being the main tool of the farmers' training and education through audio-visual methods, will include such improved practices as seeds, fertilisers, improved agricultural implements and machinery, soil conditioners, plant protection etc.

Some of the considerations which the planners and decision makers for agricultural development at the national level may take into account in regard to farmers training are as follows :

(i) The content of the farmers' training should be such as can clearly establish the fact that it is a strong instrument for making agriculture a better and more profitable business.

(ii) It should be recognised that agriculture varies from one area to another, even from one field to another. The farmers training programme, therefore, should be fitted to the local conditions. It should develop a local or regional bias and no rigid pattern should be laid down.

(iii) Training to farmers hitherto had been imparted mostly by bottomline workers in the extension hierachy, i.e., the gramsevaks or the agricultural assistants. By and large, this had not been a satisfactory arrangement. The farmers are experienced and known their problems well. They should be handled by expert group of technicians.

(iv) Radio and Television are being closely associated in the farmers' Trainining and Education Programme. India being a vast country, radio and television are perhaps the most important media to disseminate information about latest farm technology. Besides these media, other local media should be used more and more in the Farmers' Training and Education Programme.

(v) Group of farmers orgnised on a voluntary basis must provide the necessary forum to highlight the problems of the village to the technicians and disseminate the information on modern technology among the rural community.

The functioning of extension activities depends to a large degree on the organisational solutions found for this work. Themes of importance are the overall structure of extension agencies, the internal organisational patterns, such as line of command and authority, position of subject-matter specialists, communication patterns within the agency, the position of extension within the "agricultural knowledge system", i.e., between researchers and farmers, the relation to the general administration and to other service organisations.

In most of the developing countries in Africa and Asia where intervention societies play a major role, farmers' training as well as low-and medium-level staff training is carried out mostly by government agencies. Since they are commodity based, they provid job-oriented specialized knowledge for both categories. Besides, the Ministry of Agriculture may have its own staff training institutions, but normally not for farmers. Where an extension system with a unified service and mobilization of local resources exists, all training, except academic education, is the responsibility of the extension service.

Extension Resources and Staff Motivation

There have been many complaints in the past decades that the extension services, in view of their enormous task, are insufficiently staffed and that they lack adequate working facilities and finance to cover the recurrent costs. Although the data available are rather fragmentary, it can be shown that the situation is not unsatisfactory in every respect.

Extension work under conditions prevailing in Africa and Asia is a personnel-intensive task. Direct contacts between well-trained officers and their clients are necessary in many instances. The manpower problem has a quantitative and a qualitative aspect.

Further, the effectiveness of an extension service depends to a noticeable degree also on the morale and the motivation of its staff. In order to be efficient, the staff need acceptable working conditions, incentives, such as achievement-oriented pay and promotion opportunities and good staff management.

Certainly the living conditions of field agents are often difficult. It is true in most of the developing countries. They stay in villages which may not have many of the facilities of modern civilization, such as electricity, running water, cultural events, hospitals, or good schooling for their children. Many of them are separated from their families. Another problem is the pay. In many countries extension field agents are on a rather low salary grade. Incentive payments are rarely provided in government services. These aspects require immediate attention. And the staff of the extension service must be provided with better salary, perks and other incentives so that they get motivated to discharge better services to the clients.

The Farmer and his Relation to Extension and Training

There are three important factors which influence the extension work in most of the countries. They are agricultural, educational and social structures.

One of the problems with which all extension services have to cope with is the heterogeneity of agriculture. There is a considerble range of farm holding sizes and of the wealth and market orientation of farmers to be found in the various regions and groups—all of which require from extension agencies a differentiated approach if they want to satisfy their clients' specific needs. With respect to technical and economic recommendations and content of training it also makes a great difference whether the land is mainly rainfed or irrigated. Another important variable is the educational level of the farming population. It is usually taken for granted that it is easier for extension and training egencies to work with well-educated farmers than with illiterate ones who are unacquainted with the scientific background of modern farming. The inter-relationship between educational level and openness to change and contacts with extension is perhaps more complicated than it might appear at first. Certainly farmers with a good general and agricultural education have to be treated quite differently from those with little or no formal education. It is fact that from country and very often also within the countries themselves, a wide range of different levels of literacy is to be found. Training, therefore must be as per the farmers' background and understanding.

There is also a number of external structural factors influencing extension and training activities. One of them is the settlement structure. In areas with a high density of farms and village-type settlements it is easier and most cost saving to maintain personal contacts between extension officers and farmers than in thinly populated regions with a scattered settlement pattern. The road system also plays a considerable role. Where the roads are mainly untarred, the extension officers have great difficulty, atleast in the rainy season, in coping with a stringent schedule of visits to farmers.

Main Activities of Extension Services

The most important task for extension agencies is to advise farmers, male and female, on farm and home matters. This can be accomplished either by a dialogue between the extension agent and an individual discussion between one or more extension agents and a group. In both cases the objectives are to inform and educate. Extension, although not the source of information on agricultural problems and possibilities, is one of the most important systems by which farmers' aspirations are met. The extension agent can, better than the mass media, select the kind of information essential for his clients. The educational task is usually classified as non-formal education: to provide selected types of learning to particular subgroups and this is outside the framework of the formal system. A skillful extension agent will lead the farmer(s) systematically through the various phases of the adoption process : awareness of a new practice; raising of interest and motivation; first evaluation with any analysis of advantages and disadvantages; trial (if possible small scale); second evaluation. and finally the adoption.

From a semantic point of view, there are no hard and fast definitions of the terms "extension" and "training" to distinguish clearly one from the other. Extension activities are often presented as training and training courses for farmers certainly also serve extension purposes. Training has, in the words of Coombs and Ahmed, (1974) "a different basic educational tradition and philosophy, more closely allied to institutionalized schooling. In contrast to the extension approach which emphasizes the communication of information about innovative technical practices, the training approach emphasizes more systematic and deeper learning of specific basic skills and related knowledge. Training programmes typically involve assembling learners in a training centre".

3. Constraints in Agricultural Extension and Training

In a critical review of the chances and problems of farmers' training programmes it should first be pointed out that they are costly. Normally, in most of the conutries no fees are levied from trainees who belong to small farmers' communities. In some countries farmer's training is totally free irrespective of their land holdings.

It is, therefore, important to define the target groups accurately. Preference should be to young men or girls who may become group or village leaders and who do not yet have permanent obligations at home. also, in the selection of adults for training, potential leadership capacity is usually considered. In countries in which a major number of large farms or government stations exist, the training of specialized labourers is necessary too.

It is much easier to reach many farmers through training programmes with short courses. These are rightly emphasized as part of the extension programmes of most countries. Attention has to be paid, in the planning and implementation of short courses, to the following points :

* Training has to be appropriately timed, ie., it should be held mainly during slack periods and never during farm labour peaks;
* Preferably those subjects should be chosen which are of immediate relevance to farmers in the approaching agricultural season;
* The content must be adapted to the needs of a specific target group;
* Short course training should preferably be offered to men and women who are in a position to pass on what they have learned to others.

There are several constraints in farmers' training on different heads as reported by various extension personnel and extension reseerch scientists working in several Third World Countries. Further, the extent and magnitude of the problems vary country to country. However, an attempt has been made to consolidate and document these constraints from the various reports and studies and presented below. It is expected, if these constraints are taken care of or removed the agricultural extension and training can play significant roles in agricultural and rural development in the developing countries.

Constraints of Farmers' Training at Field Level

1. Training Nesds of Farmers :

(a) No farmer participation or representation in decision making on training needs and programmes,

(b) Ineffective communication of farmers' needs through the extension organizations.

(c) Political distance of small and marginal farmers is reinforced by basing their rewards on affiliation with the ruling party or government administration.

(d) Social distance of extension workers in relation to the rural society is reinforced by stationing them away from villages. And as a result they do not discharge their duties effectively.

2. Appropriate Technology Generation :

(a) Often agricultural research is oriented more to technical than to socio-economic aspects of application.

(b) The activities of research and extension at the field level are compartmentalized rather than interdependent.

(c) Lack of identification of research priorities and research allocation are insufficient.

(d) Investment behaviour of decision makers tends to be guided by big land owners and political bosses which is detrimental to rural economy.

3. Training of Trainers :

(a) Extension is oriented to piece-meal, isolated activities instead of the sequential, repetitive process of learning.

(b) Lack of focus on training has an inter-dependent component of research extension system.

(c) Policy is oriented to provide lower quality training to extension workers, closer to field level.

(d) Goal conflict and duplication of activities among the various agencies involved in training.

(e) Sharp variances in salary scale and promotional aspects among private agricultural agencies, training institutes and Universities.

(f) Lack of incentives and rewards to agricultural officers and extension workers, in particular.

(g) Non-objective criteria in recruiting staff for further training.

(h) Inadequate supervision of training and extension activities at the field level.

(i) Lack of political will to extend training and job opportunities for women in the field of agricultural extension as opposed to home economic extension.

(j) Programmes and activities are designed more for subject matter than for problem solving training.

(k) Training of extension workers is to attend and diversity to be effectively applied at field level.

(l) Lack of competent trainers and instructors and failure to attract them.

4. Facilities for Training :

(a) Training facilities are inadequate and also failure to utilise extension facilities.

(b) Unsuitability of residential centres for farmers training.

(c) Fields of the research institutes are not utilized for training purposes.

(d) Provision of facilities are not integrated with field application.

5. Reaching the small farmers :

(a) The political machinery is biased mostly in favour of big farmers, land lords and the influencials.

(b) The "trickle-down" approach of extension programme through farm leaders who are chosen on the basis of political loyalty rather than their innovative role.

(c) Farmers are not organised always as special interest groups.

(d) Farmers' needs for training in specific skills are not a basis for recruitment to training activities.

(e) Lack of focus on the main target groups because of the absence of economists and sociologists from extension and training centres.

(f) Small farmers are not motivated to participate in training because the land tenancy and credit structures are not geared to help them implement what they learn.

(g) Lack of incentives to productive workers.

6. Appropriate Methods of Training :

(a) Methods are oriented to individual rather than group training.

(b) Policy is oriented to theorising rather than testing and developing alternative methods of extension and training.

(c) Lack of organizational support to extension workers to implement group methods at field level.

(d) Scheduling of training and extension activities over a long period of time and away from farmers' homes reduces farmers' participation.

(e) Methods are often manipulated to coerce farmers rather than develop their ability to choose.

(f) Farmers are not provided with enough opportunities and facilities of practising new skills.

(g) The primacy of extension workers role in farmers training is not effectively supported.

(h) Institutes and instructors attempt to control and inhibit farmers' thinking and action and lead them to adjust to their environment rather than transform it.

7. Follow up of application of learned skills :

(a) The task of evaluation of training and extension activities is not organisationally integrated in the programme cycle.

(b) Extension worker' contribution to increased productivity of farmers is not linked to a system of incentives which motivates them to monitor application of skills by farmers.

(c) Supervising farmers after the initial phase of applying a new skills is not carried out regularly and with a view to correcting the un-desired behaviour.

(d) Inputs are either not provided to farmers or provided too late to be used.

(e) Lack of proper documentation of programme inputs and outputs.

(f) Credit institutions cater more for the needs of the commercial sector than they do for the needs of small and marginal farmers.

(g) Lack of support to group farming.

References

Coombs, P.H. and Ahmed, M. 1974. *Attacking Rural Poverty—How Norformal Education Can Help*, Baltimore and London, Johns Hopkins University Press.

Sudad, S.H. 1980, *Major Constraints in Farmer Training at Field Level, Studies from Jordon, Malaysia and Tanzania*—A Research Report, Rome, FAO.

Von Blackenburg, P. 1984. *Agricultural Extension Systems in Some African and Asian Countries.* FAO Economic and Social Development Paper-46, Rome, FAO.

SIX

Agricultural Extension Challenges in India—What Can Be Done ?

Transfer of research results and adoption of developed agricultural technology by farmers and other clientele groups have always been major constraints in agricultural and rural development in India. It has been varyingly estimated that only 25-40% of developed technology ever get adopted by the farmers. The multitude of the reasons such as relevance of the technology, input constraints, lack of knoweldge and inadequacy of the transfer of technology systems etc., have been indicated as the maladies. It is difficult to pin-point which particular reason is more responsible in non-adoption of the technologies by the farmers but one reason which is accepted widely that the transfer of technology system should be improved to bridge the gap between technology developed and technology adopted.

In this regard, it is not out of the place to say that Indian Agricultural Research has achieved some significant breakthrough in developing appropriate research to contribute to its vast agricultural development. It has set up a maga research effort and has built-up organisations with about 30,000 professional scientists and large number of supporting staff, a vast net work of attendant research and extension education groups and a very substantial annual budget of several million rupees. The conceptual understanding of the research community is high and they have impeccable credentials. However, the out-put of the system is considered to be not as high as is expected from such vast resources and potential. Many critics of the system have pointed out that these research efforts have increased regional disparties, added to ecological degradation, promoted high cost and high energy agriculture and have added to problems of land and water management, besides widening the distances between the researcher and the farmers with poor endowments.

Therefore, if agricultural research is to be useful, it should take into account the following four suggestions :

1. Identification of the relevant research system and developing a valid project.
2. Developing a technology option with a valid solution.
3. Stand the regours of a field trial as proof of social cost effectiveness.
4. Wider adoption of the farm level as indication of societal acceptance.

Further, the experiences of last four decades of extension activities in the field of agriculture and rural development in India have clearly indicated that extension is one of the weak links in agricultural development in the country. There are several questions raised for the purpose by many social scientists, agricultural development experts and planners in the national level. Considering all of their view points in this regard following issues on extension can be putforth for discussion for finding out new strategy of extension and/or transfer of technology.

Issues on Agriculturual Extension

1. In India overall extension activities are done by State Agricultural Universities (SAU), State Department of

Agriculture and Indian Council of Agriculture Research (ICAR) with a little variation and each organisation is independent for the purpose in theoretical sense.

2. The word "extension activity" used in relation to the SAU and the State Government does not perhaps mean the same thing. ICAR is mostly involved in frontline extension activities with its four transfer of technology projects namely, National Demonstration (ND), Krishi Vigyan Kendra (KVK) and Trainers" Training Centre (TTC), Operational Research Project (ORP) and Lab to Land Programme (LLP).

3. There are distinct difference in extension function between Agricultural University and State Government. The following table highlights the differences between the two extension efforts.

Agricultural University	*State Government*
— Feedback machanism for sharper Research focus	The main vehicle for verticle technology transfer.
— A technical support to the State Government	Supplier of subsidised inputs to farmers.
— Shares knowledge with farmers, State Government employees	The administrative buffer between the farming community and State.
— A mini extension system in the University catchment area.	First level client for SAU research.

4. The relation between University and the State Government has many facets. State Government is a major provider of funds for the university and also cooperating agency for technology transfer. There is a status-knowledge gap between the two groups. In some ways

State Government is administrative superior than the University. In this circumstances, inter-relations for effective transfer of technology are crucial. Not only good relations but an institutional compatibility is required for effective transfer of technology between University and State Government.

5. There is a little confusion about the place of extension in SAU set-up. The Director of Extension is not able to devote required time for Agricultural extension in the field. Extension programmes generally receive casual attention at all levels of the University. Staff recruited to conduct extension work in KVK are not oriented to village work. Further, prolonged postings of any faculty member in extension activity may stagnate his her professional growth. Therefore, there is, perhaps an urgent need to redefining the scope of extension in SAUs and man them appropriately.

6. Another question raised by many social Scientists that whether the extension work need soclal conflict resolution skills in addition to technology knowledge ? How does the SAUs provide it to them ? It is an area where SAUs knowledge is perhaps limited. Therefore, redefining of university extension is must.

7. Effective learning is an interaction between the older tradition of farm practice and the modern trend of scientific inquiry each reacting to the other as two equally important perception of reality. This would need an attitudinal change as much as a structural reorganisation. Should SAUs also have hard core extension responsibilities like the land grant colleges of USA ?

8. Technology in agriculture has two parts-improved verities which encapsulate yield capabilities and recommended optimal practice with which the farmer takes

liberties choosing some. Rejecting others, should extension methodologies deal with each differently ? Also does research for the resource poor farmers needed distinct approach and whether that could be the responsibility of University Extension ?

Therefore, the soundness of technology generation process—prioritisation and formulation of research programmes, testing of technologies, farmer acceptability etc., are most important to be considered before technology generation and dissemination of the developed technology to the farmers for its adoption. Also it is to be kept in mind that three distrinct sets of actors namely, Scientists, Manager of the System and Farmers are involved in technology generation and dissemination. And whether management principles can be applied for improving the effectiveness of these three sets of actors in their work output ?

Keeping this in view this chapter has been designed to highlight the various challenges ahead in Agricultural Extension in India and the possible solutions to meet those with three heads, namely :

1. Current Agricultural Research Scenario in India frcm Extension View Point;
2. Agricultural Extension System—A Retrospect; and
3. Agricultural Extension for 21st Century—Some Issues.

1. Current Agricultural Research Scenario in India From Extension View Point

The Agricultural Research Scenario of India over the last fourty years since independence has some significant breakthrough and growth in various fields. These developments can be grouped in nutshall on following ten heads, namely :

1. The Problem
2. Post Green Revolution Concerns,

3. Perceptional Congruence,
4. Some Imperatives,
6. Four Streams of Research Endeavour,
6. Focussing Research Report,
7. Profile of a Modified Technology Generation Strategy,
8. Understanding the User,
9. Anatomy of a Technical Solution, and
10. Structural Issues.

The lessons can be taken from these to make significant breakthrough in research and extension linkages which are needed quitely to-day for effective dissemination of research results to its users.

1. The Problem

The Indian Agricultural Research has achieved some significant breakthrough with its mega research efforts by 30 thousands scientists, a vast network of teaching, research and extension systems and an annual budget of Rs. 100 crores of rupees. But the productivity of the same is low, though conceptual understanding of the research community is high. Therefore, question comes what is the problem ?

2. Post-Green Revolution Concerns

Green Revolution Strategies which have a bias in favour of resource rich farmers have solved some problems but added many more. It has not given any answer or solution to the 60 million resource poor farmers or 300 million people. Factually, it has increased the regional disparities, had added to the ecological degradation, promoted high cost, high energy agriculture and also added to water management problems.

Now India needs a socially, economically responsible research strategy for better farming systems to solve integrated problems.

3. *Perceptional Congruence*

Three distinct sets of personnel are involved in technology generation and dissemination, namely, scientists, managers of the system and farmers. Each one has a point of view. Interesting examples may be cited in this regard as mentioned bleow :

Scientist	*System Manager*	*Farmer*
—Peer recognition	—National Vs local concern	—Has unique risk perceptions
—Bias towards number oriented problems and where succes is more likely	—Compulsions of size —Policy imperatives —Administrative overburden	—Acts as a member of a group —Not easily taken in
—A 'telling' rather than a 'listening' culture		
—Personal advancement		

But it is not considered for generating technology and building system to disseminate it. Therefore, research paradigm need to consciously achieve perceptional congruence.

4. *Some Imperatives*

To make agricultural research useful it should pass through four stages namely, research project, technology option, field trial and then farm practice. No single one is independent and the four are to be seen in wholesum for better research knowledge generation and the research output dissemination to its users. Particularly, the second one i.e., technology option is more important. Further, the present failure for agricultural research generation and project formulation to societal acceptance of farm practices is due to inability to understand the problem-inability to find a solution which is cost effective and inability to market it to the target groups.

5. *Four Streams of Research Endeavour*

There are four distinct streams of agricultural research which together provide the basis of research agenda of 1990s in India.

(a) Continuation of Research which is aimed at the resource rich farmers and their problems.

(b) Identifying the concerns of resource poor farmers;

(c) Blue skies research which a University ambience can offer and;

(d) Enquiry and evaluation of way out farming systems like "do nothing farming" or "perma culture."

6. *Focussing Research Effort*

The future research thrust should be on farming systems in specific agro-climatic zones. A sea change is required for institutions where primacy was of the discipline.

Also market driven consumption oriented farm systems need to deal with significantly, different externalities, and agricultural research needs an institutional interface with industrial and engineering research institutions : in horticulture, implements, even in crops like oilseeds.

7. *Profile of a Motivated Technology Generation Strategy*

If agricultural research is a continum from new varieties, and improved agricultural practice to post-harvest technology—diversity of resource endowments, market-structures further multiples available options. Therefore, the strategy is to choose desired societal change and social engineering must be the end and technology should be the one of the means to achieve it. This would mean writing research brief which incorporates scientific and social objectives.

8. *Understanding the User*

The concept of a progressive farmer as an opposite of a late adopter perhaps is passe. The consumer needs to be convinced with what he has offered in technology is worthwhile for him as he sees it.

When one decides to market ideas rather than hand them down understanding the user assumes critical importance.

9. *Anatomy of a Technological Solution*

Agricultural research offers basically a three part solution to farmer problems—a better variety, a most effective pratice and essential inputs. Together or each of them improves the return to the farmer. Further, the solution mix chosen by the farmer depends on his endowments and risk perceptions.

10. *Structural Issues*

For whatever reason the agricultural research establishment is a large complex system—with the burden of princples, a wide band of skill mix, nonmisceble cultures, conflicting stakeholder interest and geographical spread.

This makes the motivation, reward and punishment system difficult and achieving integration of teaching, research and extension education becomes more complex. Here, question comes—can successful corporate management practice which is familiar with large systems be of some use ?

And lastly, with this critical analysis of agricultural research and its several dimensions it is urgently needed now to rejuvinate our research and extension systems so that the suitable technology generated by the modified research systems will be disseminated effectively through further, modified extension system for better adoption and use by the farmers.

2. Agricultural Extension System—A Retrospect

Since independence (1947), Government of India (GOI) has given high priority to rural development, for its nearly 80% of the population live in villages. Agriculture has been the major occupation of the rural people (70%) and, therefore, agriculture is the mainstream of Indian economy.

There are four extension organizational streams which contribute to transfer of technology for agricultural and rural development :

(a) First-line extension system of the ICAR;

(b) The Community Development Programme and Training and Visit System being promoted by the Ministry of Agriculture, Government of India;

(c Rural Development Projects of the Department of Rural Development, Ministry of Agriculture, Government of India; and

(d) Non-government organizations/voluntary efforts.

Fig. 1 shows the operational mechanisms and relationship among various functionaries of the extension system. For details, only first-line extension system of the ICAR is being discussed (Fig. 2).

First-line Extension System

The first-line extension education role is mainly the institutional role to promoting science and technology in agriculture the agricultural universities (26) and the ICAR Research Institutes (41) are the main partners in this system.

This system aims at :

(i) promptly demonstrating the latest agricultural technologies to the farmers as well as the extension functionaries of the State Departments of Agriculture, so that

Fig.1 TRANSFER OF TECHNOLOGY SYSTEM IN INDIA

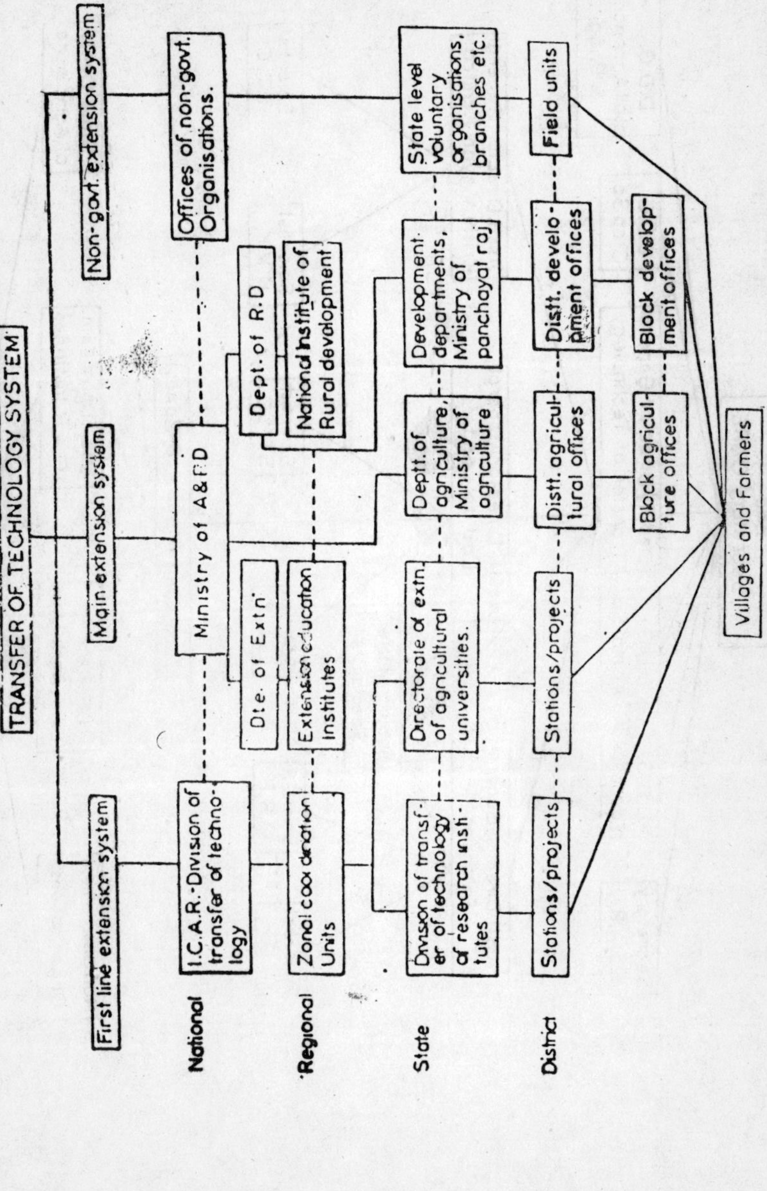

Fig.2 TRANSFER OF TECHNOLOGY DIVISION IN THE I.C.A.R. SYSTEM

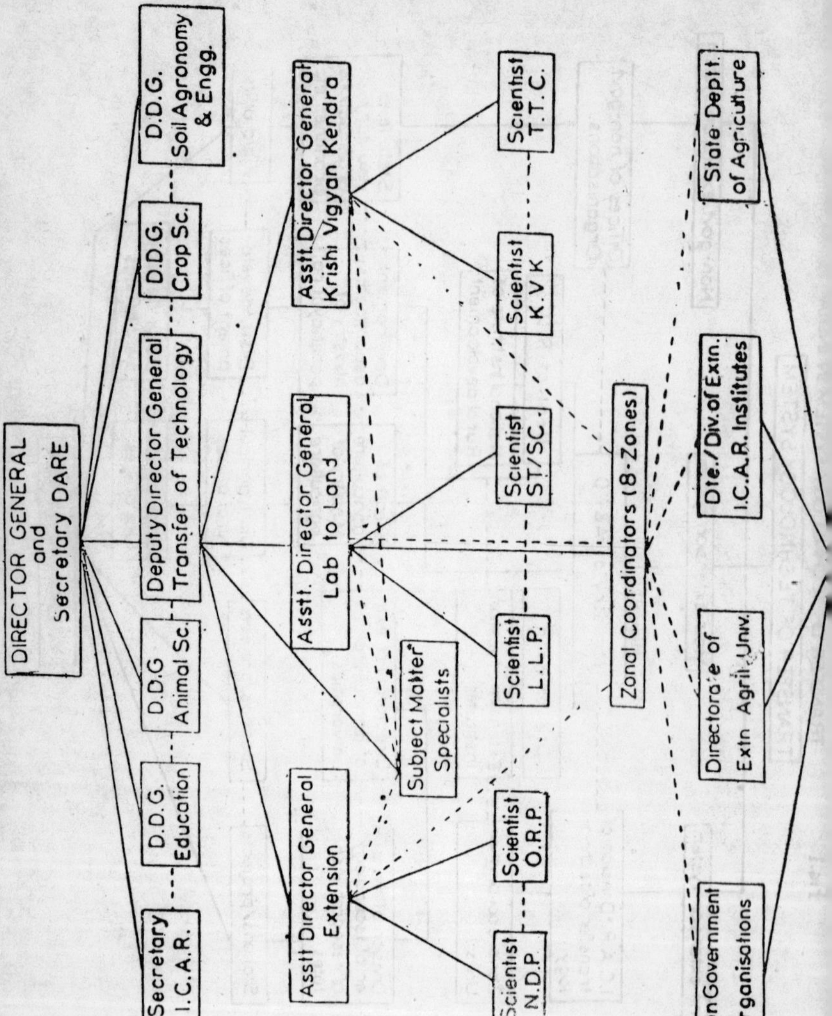

time-lag between generation of technologies and their adoption is reduced;

(ii) verifying and testing the technologies in socio-economic condition of the farmers;

iii) getting first hand scientific feed-back for improving the relevance of research, education and training; and

(v) conducting researches is relation to socio-economic implications of transfer of technology.

Besides the limited extension programme of each agricultural institutions including Agricultural Universities and ICAR Research Institutes, there are four major first-line extension projects launched by the ICAR namely :

(a) National Demonstrations in 48 districts—sites keeps on changing every six years;

(b) Operational Research Projects in 152 centres—keeping on changing sites every five years;

(c) Krishi Vigyan Kendras (Farm Science Centres) in 91 districts; and

(d) Lab-to-Land Programme in 101 centres in existing institutions and projects. The detailed organization of the Division of Extension in the ICAR is presented in Fig. 3.

Research-Education-Extension Linkages

The projects have been showing the genetic production potential of the improved varieties as well as the management practices and training the farmers as well as the extension functionaries. They have been also serving as the feedback machanisms for the scientists/institutions. The catalytic role of these projects and the agricultural institutions have been of great value for the other extension systems which have the main mandate for transfer of technology and accelerating agricultural production.

Fig. 3. Organisation of the Division of Extension in the ICAR (Simplified)

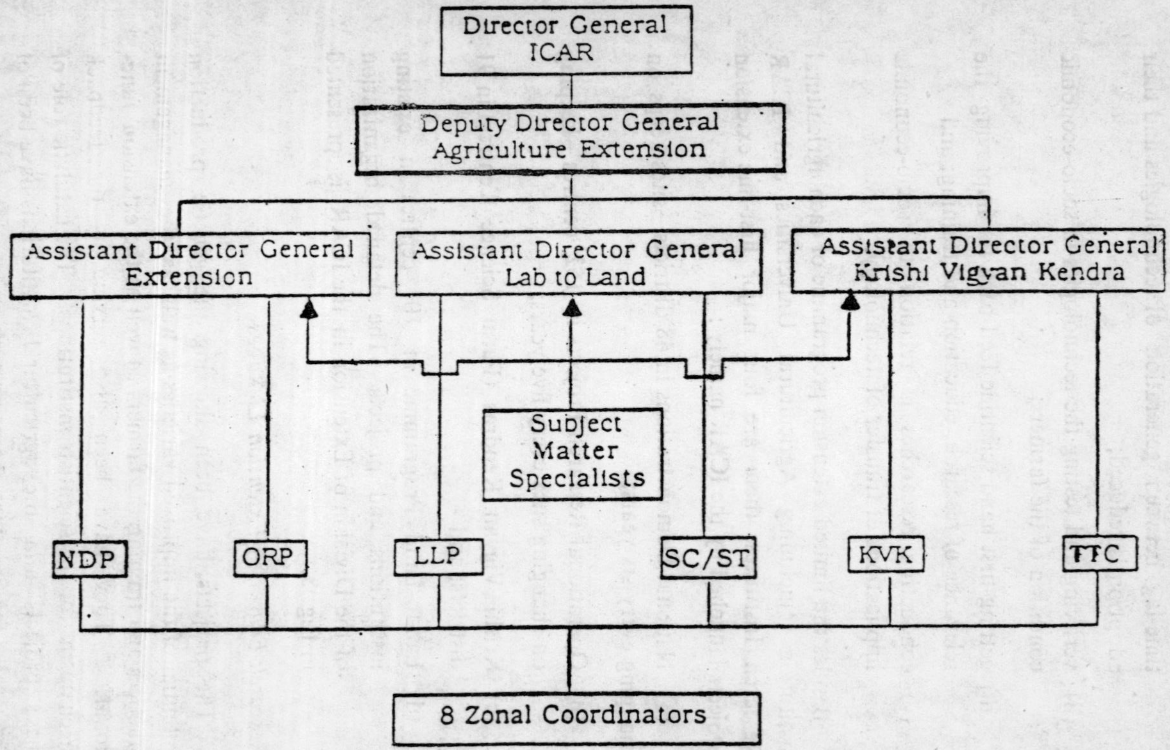

Note ; Zonal Coordinators liaise with SAUs, ICAR Institutes, State Departments of Agriculture and NGOs.

The first-line extension education role has its root in the U.S. Land Grant Pattern of Education where State Universities have the full responsibility for extension education in agriculture, and the State Departments of Agriculture are responsible for input support and supply. The pattern of integrated functioning of education, research and extension was introduced in India in 1960 when the establishment of Agricultural Universities were launched on the model of the USA. Now there are 26 Agricultural Universities and all have strong Directorate of Extension Education for first-line extension programmes. Since 1960, they have played a major role in technology generation, manpower development and extension education.

The ICAR Research Institutes are basically devoted to research in their specialized areas. But the concept of integrated working being so rewarding, the ICAR has promoted this approach to ICAR Research Institutes also. For instance, the three National Institutes i.e. IARI* (New Delhi), NDRI* (Karnal), and IVRI* (Izatnagar) have a strong wing of Transfer of Technology headed by a Joint Director in each (better ranked than the Directors of Extension of SAUs). In case of other Institutes, there are Departments/Cells of Extension Education; they are further being strengthened to be more effective in promoting the relevant research findings in the interest of accelerating their technologies in the context of cropping/farming systems prevalent in their respective areas.

Manpower in Agricultural Extension and Technology Transfer

In India agricultural extension efforts are pursued by the Union (national) and state (nation wide) public sectors commodity extension activities carried out by the private sector, and numerous agricultural and rural development activities undertaken by voluntary non-governmental organisations (NGOs).

* IARI : Indian Agricultural Research Institute.
** NDRI : National Dairy Research Institute.
*** IVRI : Indian Veterinry Reseaarch Institute.

India to-day has a highly developed network of agricultural extension with a large contingent of staff spread across the nation. According to published, albeit, symewhat dated, calculations (Swanson and Rassi, 1981), there were about 71,834 VEWs, some 18,044 AEOs, some 1,895 SMSs, some 5,090 SDEOs and Assistant SDEOs, some 2,000 DAOs and Assistant DAOs, and some 500 state-level Joint Directors and Additional Directors of Agriculture in the states and territories in 1981, at which time T & V was operating in only nine states. Given the expansion of the system to 15 states by April 1986 and that the Swanson-Rassi list does not include APCs (Agricultural Production Commissioners). Secretaries and Additional Secretaries, we may roughly calculate that there are at the middle and top levels some 2,500 to 3,000 officials.

The T & V system with its built-in training and retraining components for functionaries at the field level and for middle level cadres, provides popular and need-based training programmes organized in keeping with the need for timely and local-specific technological information. Grassroots VEWs are mandated to provide periodic technical information to farmers. For middle-level personnel the Department of Extension (DOE) has developed a number of Extension Education Institute (EEIs), as already mentioned herein, and these are being utilized for imparting subject matter training as well as extension and management training for the SMS and other middle-level personnel. T & V training for higher level officials in the agricultural extension network has been limited to monthly (zonal) and seasonal workshops on technical matters.

With this background of vast agricultural extension network of the country and the manpower available for the purpose there is ample opportunity to disseminate the research results to its users effectively if all aspects of technology transfer process are scientifically managed. Further, considering the capability and potentiality of the existing research-extension linkage system and the agricultural extension challenges of the 21st century, it can be well said that the present system is set for better synthesis of research results into its utilization. Only dynamism and clearcut objectives are necessary to achieve this.

3. Agricultural Extension for 21st Century—Some Issues

The discipline, extension is unique in its structure and func-function. Interestingly, it has not been restricted to a single programme or activity like most other disciplines, but rather, has been allowed to adjust changing needs of the situation, time and individuals in the society. Society has allowed few organisations this flexibility. Organisations tend to be created for a single purpose, but extension has defined its role as education, even though the subject matter and audience have changed over time and place. Therefore, extension as a discipline has a typical distinct identity. Now time has come, we have to think how can we better the effectiveness of this extension to achieve our cherished goal of developing agriculture.

To meet the challenges of agricultural development in 21st Century, there is an urgent need to change the structure and function of agricultural extension. To make agricultural extension a more viable and efficient tool of technology transfer following important issues must be considered. So that it can be meaningful to cope-up with the changing situation of agriculture in 21st century.

Issues on Agricultural Extension

1. Decentralised Extension : Present top-down management decision making in agricultural extension generally result in ineffective extension systems. In both programmes and operations such systems are characterised by decisions made by a few people at the top which generally are not effectively implemented and carried out by most people at the bottom. And as a result, extension suffers. In top-down systems of decision making in extension, decisions may not only be too slow in coming, but they are likely to suffer in quality because of decisions made on inadequate information about local conditions.

Therefore, it is widely suggested by various extension experts throughout the world that decentralised extension brings better and purposful results.

Extension managers may not understand options and may be more comfortable with the current system of top-down management. They may also feel that they cannot risk decentralisation because they would not be supported from top when problems occur because of delegation. But this is the need and we must bring the change. It is true that changing, from a top-down authoritarian management style to a decentralised stlye, the functions through delegation, involvement, and interaction is complex process but if sincere efforts are made by all the concerned in the system, no doubt, it will be easier and possible.

2. *Farmer to Farmer Extension* : Enough has been talked, suggested, advised and widely discussed about how to make the most effective and efficient linkages with farmers for technology transfer over the years throughout the world, but not much is said till to date about farmer to farmer extension as a mode of dissemination of agricultural information.

The farmers have active communication networks linked by groups and individuals. So both content and mode of communication are present and widely used by them to adopt technologies, the farmers believe, are affordable and readily available, reduce risk, generate more income, save labour and fit into their farming practices. Learning from other farmers is more common than learning from researchers and extensionsits because very few technologies come directly from this latter sources. In this farmer to farmer extension a multipliar effect is achieved through the group process, peer opinion, testimony and demonstration through networks like cooperatives, young farmers' club, women's groups and other farmers' service societies.

Hence, it is important to put into practice and encourage the farmer to farmer extension for effective transfer of agricultural knowledges. This also supports the view of puting the farmer in the feedback loops with research and extension and allowing participation in trials of new technologies and in more experimentation for self help.

3. *Effective Management in Extension System* : Designing and introducing the right and suitable system of extension is important and need to be periodically reviewed and adapted to the changing situations. There is also need of a strong research support for this periodical comprehensive rcview of the functioning of the system. So far these aspects were not given much importance by decision makers and planners of agricultural extension.

4. *Policy and Funding Support for Extension* : If we want the extension system to work more efficiently there should be continnous policy and funding support from the policy makers and the Government. The perceptions of the policy makers also should be changed regarding the functioning of the extension system. Most of the time their perceptions are unfavourable because of inadequate understanding of the process of opinion formation. Perhaps, there is a lack of proper exposure and articulation about the contribution of extension to agricultural development. It is true that agricultural extension has significant contribution in the development of agriculture particularly in the area of economic growth, employment generation, poverty alleviation etc. But there is a dearth of written, documented research data on these aspects. These are to be taken into consideration and authentic document on contribution of agricultural extension in agriculture development are to be prepared. Therefore, more studies are to be undertaken in this direction.

5. *Image of Agricultural Extension*: Generally there is a poor image of agricultural extension in the mind of most of the development experts, policy makers and top level administrative functionaries in most of the countries in the third world. This is to be changed. It is because most of the policy markers and top administrative experts form their opinions about extension systems and the agricultural extension discipline through interacting extension functionaries. Most of the time these extension functionaries are not articulate and fails to present their cases to the experts effectively and a better image of agricultural extension is not formed. So there is an urgent need to make an effective attempt to sensitise the extension functionaries at all levels for creating better image of agricultural extension.

6. *Organisational Structure and Renewal*: Every extension is designed to meet the objectives at given time but over a period of changes in social, cultural and economic aspects of the individuals in the society the objectives of the extedsion systems are to be redesigned which are not done in most of the cases before and as a result extension objectives are not met. The periodical review, therefore, is required to see the extension system is compatible with the current objectives as per changes in the society.

Further, to make the extension more effective and meaningful a functional organisational structure is essential. This is more important when extension system is a part of the overall organisational structure of the agricultural departments. Often, while extension strategy and objectives change simultaneous changes are not brought in the functional organisational structure of the department and as a result functions of whole system suffer. Therefore, it is suggested that an effective linkage must be there within the organisational structure and at its various levels of hierarchy. Also the organisation should have purposeful systems and procedures to ensure adequate decentralisation of administrative and financial powers for effective functioning of its various units.

In most of the extension organisational systems functional job charts are not prepared meaningfully for its various functionaries and personnel. These job charts would be meaningful only if the job content is feasible and significant with reference to technical competence and span of control of the functionaries. So the functional job chart is must for every extension worker irrespective of his/her position in the organisation. Often it is seen that there is a much variation in the purpose and understanding of different functionaries in extension system. Why this happens is to be examined. Whether educational qualification, experience, training, motivation and positive attitude towards the job have any significance for the better performance of the extension worker are to be studied. And then only different personnel is to be appointed and posted for different kinds of work. This definitely, will bring more effectiveness in the working of the extension system.

7. *Training of Extension Personnel*: Training is a most important component for improving the skill to perform better among agricultural extension personnel. There are number of training Institutes to impart training to this effect in the country. But most of the time we over-look whether, these training Institutes are suitably equipped to impart the training to the extension personnel : whether, there is a system to assess the quality of training with reference to job performance of the trainees ? Whether, training capsules are based on the evaluation of the training programme, training institutes and the performance of the trainees ? Further, whether, trainers of the training institutes are capable of imparting proper training to the trainees ? Whether, they can perform better in job situations than the trainees ?. How much credibility the trainers have established in performing their job effectively ? These questions are to be answered and looked into for making training programme effective, meaningful and purposeful. And these would inturn help the trained agricultural extension personnel to contribute maximum in developing agricultural extension system to achieve its goal.

8. *Reward and Punishment* : In the effective management system the employees in the organisation must be accountable for their job performances. The individual should be rewarded if he achieves the goal of the task assigned to him. Again, the individual should get punishment too if he fails to achieve that objective in a given time. And then only the system in organisation work. This reward and punishment system helps the individuals working in the organisation to achieve their personal goal and satisfy their own needs. Simultaneously it also helps the organisation to achieve its goal and objective with the support of the individuals working in that organisation.

This system of incentive could be detrimental and disfunctional again if it is not considered fair by the employees. The assessment for providing incentive to some-one for his achievement or giving punishment for his poor performance should be proper and accepted mostly by others. Not only good performers will get rewards and incentives but also poor performers should get some incentives to over-come their poor performance. The assessment in this regard may be difficult and critical but should be done with caution.

9. *Supervision and Guidance* : Supervision and guidance are they key functions of the manager of any system. In extension system these two aspects are often lacking and as a result the functionaries at all levels of hierarchy are not doing their best to achieve the set objectives.

A sub-system must be evolved within the system of extension by which the functionaries of every level are properly guided and supervised for their work on technical aspects, on their needs and aspirations, on constraints in their work and on possible solutions to that effect. And these supervisions by senior officers in the field are central to the functioning of an extension system. And whether this system is working or not, a review on regular interval should be done to see its continuity.

10. *The Support and Service Systems* : For the success of extension system, support and services sub-systems are must,

The only transfer of agricultural knowledge will not bring success in adoption of technology, unless it is supported with required input supplies. Most of the time, agricultural extension strategy fails and rate of adoption of agricultural technology does not increase because, the technology generated and disseminated to the farmers for its adoption are without support and services of inputs needed for its adoption.

Therefore, research-extension linkage, is important for effective transfer of technology and its adoption by the clientele. There should also be a system for periodical testing of technology jointly by the extension and research functionaries for its adoption or rejection by the clientele.

If these issues are taken into account for effective transfer of technology in agricultural extension system we may not be far away to meet the challenges of agricultural extension for agricultural development in 21st century.

Reference

Swanson, B. and Rassi, J. 1981. International Directory of National Extension Systems. Urbana, IL : University of Illinois at Urbana–Champaign, Bureau of Educational Research

The only transfer of agricultural knowledge will not bring success in adoption of technology, unless it is supported with required input supplies. Most of the time the centralised extension strategy fails and rate of adoption of agricultural technology does not increase because the technology generated and disseminated to the farmers for its adoption are without support and services of inputs needed for its adoption.

Therefore, research-extension linkage, is important for effective transfer of technology and its adoption by the clientele. There should also be a system for periodical testing of technology jointly by the extension and research functionaries for its adoption or rejection by the clientele.

If these issues are taken into account for effective transfer of technology in agricultural extension system we may not be far away to meet the challenges of Agricultural extension for agricultural development in 21st century.

Reference

Swanson, B. and Rassi, J. (1981). International Directory of National Extension Systems. Urbana, Ill.: University of Illinois at Urbana-Champaign, Bureau of Educational Research.

Index